It has been said by those who have studied ___ ___ ___ has at its roots a wrong perception of God. Our age is ___ ___ rong conceptions of who God is and what He is like. One of the more common misconceptions of Him is that the God of the Old Testament is different from the God of the New, and the God of the New Testament is preferred over the God of the Old because He is more kind and merciful. In *God in His Own Image*, the author sets forth a sound theological presentation of the God of the Bible, not in academic theological terms, but with a pastoral approach that will appeal to and be easily understood by those in the pew as only a pastor can do.

SAMUEL DALLESSANDRO
East Hazel Crest Bible Church
Adjunct faculty, Moody Bible Institute

Syd Brestel has done us all a wonderful service by writing *God in His Own Image*. So many people are asking for help in answering why evil acts are committed in our society. "Where is God in all of this?" they ask. Syd not only answers the question but he helps us understand and know God more intimately. I have already used the book in ministering to people struggling with evil acts in our world.

JOHN VAWTER
Church consultant, conference speaker, author, and former president of Phoenix Seminary and Western Seminary, former northwest regional director of Campus Crusade for Christ (CRU)

If you have questioned how a God of love can also be a God of wrath, this book offers the answer found in the fullness of God's character. Syd Brestel gives new insight to the tension between God's kindness and severity (Rom. 11:22), making his case through personal experience and theological reflection. His insight has helped me embrace the harder truths of God's judgments. I recommend this book for anyone who wants to taste and see God is good.

RANDY MYER
Superintendent of the Pacific Conference of the Evangelical Church

In our grasp to understand the true nature of God, the pendulum swings back and forth between the seeming opposite character descriptions of His severity and His kindness. The casual reader of Scripture tends to conclude from the Old Testament that God is stern and severe, while they may decide that in the New Testament He is kind and forgiving. Which is He? In this timely, fresh look at the question, Syd Brestel brings the pendulum back to center by showing that in Jesus Christ we have the full and final portrayal of God, far beyond our finite understanding of both His severity and kindness. Syd, my beloved pastor, is widely known and respected as a devout lover and scholar of the Scriptures. The reader of *God in His Own Image* will be brought into deeper awe and worship of the God who is!

DOUG BARRAM
Former regional director of Young Life, volunteer in an alternative high school

This book brings to light the kindness and the severity of our God. "His love is so severe and unselfish that His Son came to live and die to pay the penalty I deserve." Syd makes it clear that every act of discipline God brings upon His people, no matter how severe, pales in comparison with the severe judgment Christ incurred at the cross. Every act of kindness that you and I receive from God is a result of God the Father's kindness toward His Son in raising Him from the dead.

MARK A. HOEFFNER
Executive Director, CB Northwest

Syd Brestel brings years of ministry experience and biblical wisdom to the paradox of the goodness of God coupled with the severity of God. In this highly accessible work of practical theology, Brestel takes the reader on a journey through the Scriptures and the lessons he's learned in his own life as he helps unpack the character and consistency of God. This book will help anyone who hungers to know God more intimately. I can't recommend it highly enough!

KEN WYTSMA
Lead pastor of Village Church and author of *Redeeming How We Talk*

Both personal spiritual growth and effective ministry to others depends upon an accurate understanding of God's self-revelation. That understanding in turn depends upon avoiding false dichotomies that reduce both/ands to either/ors. Pastoring others for nearly four decades, and following Christ for even longer than that, has well equipped Syd Brestel to write this timely book that provides an appropriately balanced and integrated understanding of God's character. I pray that it will be widely read so that we emerge with a more faithful understanding of the God to whom we relate and whom we represent.

RANDAL ROBERTS
President and Professor of Christian Spirituality, Western Seminary, Portland, OR

Mark Twain once quipped that "God made man in His own image and ever since man has been returning the favor." Our recent revisions of the divine show this tendency is alive and well today. Many affirm God's love but deny His holiness. They accept His mercy but not His judgment. In *God in His Own Image*, Syd Brestel offers a winsome corrective. Through moving stories and clear exposition of relevant Bible passages, Brestel, a seasoned pastor, reintroduces readers to the God that they've forgotten. He shows why it's important to embrace the twin attributes of God's mercy and sternness. He sketches a portrayal of God that inspires fear and wonder. He makes God big again. After turning the final page, readers will have an appreciation for God's love and holiness—and a renewed desire to bow down and worship.

DREW DYCK
Author of *Your Future Self Will Thank You: Secrets to Self-Control from the Bible and Brain Science* and *Yawning at Tigers: You Can't Tame God, So Stop Trying*

GOD
IN HIS OWN
IMAGE

Loving God for who He is . . .
not who we want Him to be

SYD BRESTEL

MOODY PUBLISHERS
CHICAGO

Some details have been changed to protect the privacy of individuals.

All Scripture quotations, unless otherwise indicated, are taken from the ESV® Bible (The Holy Bible, English Standard Version®), copyright © 2001 by Crossway, a publishing ministry of Good News Publishers. Used by permission. All rights reserved.

Scripture quotations marked (NIV) are taken from the Holy Bible, New International Version®, NIV®. Copyright © 1973, 1978, 1984, 2011 by Biblica, Inc.™ Used by permission of Zondervan. All rights reserved worldwide. www.zondervan.com The "NIV" and "New International Version" are trademarks registered in the United States Patent and Trademark Office by Biblica, Inc.™

Scripture quotations marked KJV are taken from the King James Version

Scripture quotations marked NASB are taken from the *New American Standard Bible*®, Copyright © The Lockman Foundation 1960, 1962, 1963, 1968, 1971, 1972, 1973, 1975, 1977, 1995. Used by permission.

Scripture quotations marked (NLT) are taken from the Holy Bible, New Living Translation, copyright ©1996, 2004, 2015 by Tyndale House Foundation. Used by permission of Tyndale House Publishers, Inc., Carol Stream, Illinois 60188. All rights reserved.

Scripture quotations marked (TLB) are taken from The Living Bible copyright © 1971. Used by permission of Tyndale House Publishers, Inc., Carol Stream, Illinois 60188. All rights reserved.

Scripture quotations marked *The Message* are from *The Message,* copyright © by Eugene H. Peterson 1993, 1994, 1995. Used by permission of NavPress Publishing Group.

Edited by Cheryl Molin
Interior design: Ragont Design
Cover design: Erik M. Peterson
Cover photo of burning bush copyright © 2018 by Noerpol / Lightstock (541137). All rights reserved
Author photo: Sharon Miller

Library of Congress Cataloging-in-Publication Data

Names: Brestel, Syd, author.
Title: God in His own image : loving God for who He is ... not who we want
    Him to be / Syd Brestel.
Description: Chicago : Moody Publishers, 2019. | Includes bibliographical
    references.
Identifiers: LCCN 2019000179 (print) | LCCN 2019010945 (ebook) | ISBN
    9780802497710 (ebook) | ISBN 9780802419033
Subjects: LCSH: God (Christianity) | Image of God. | God
    (Christianity)--Attributes.
Classification: LCC BT103 (ebook) | LCC BT103 .B745 2019 (print) | DDC
    231/.4--dc23
LC record available at https://lccn.loc.gov/2019000179

ISBN: 978-0-8024-1903-3

We hope you enjoy this book from Moody Publishers. Our goal is to provide high-quality, thought-provoking books and products that connect truth to your real needs and challenges. For more information on other books and products that will help you with all your important relationships, go to www.moodypublishers.com or write to:

Moody Publishers
820 N. La Salle Boulevard
Chicago, IL 60610

1 3 5 7 9 10 8 6 4 2

To Mary,

My helpmate, encourager,
and most cherished friend.

I've drunk too deeply from your cup
to e'er desire another.
I've gazed so deeply in your eyes
to realize how precious you are, my love.

Contents

Preface

Writing a book was never on my bucket list. But here I am, writing a preface, of all things.

After serving as a pastor more than forty-five years and now enjoying a busy and fulfilling retirement, why in the world would I take on something like this?

Why now? Why this book? It's simply because I have something I want very much to say about my God, and if I don't say it now . . . well then, chances are I never will.

So here goes. Are you with me?

Paul, in Romans 11:22, in the middle of a vast and wide-ranging argument about Israel and the Gentiles, uses this little phrase: "Note then *the kindness and the severity* of God. . . ." (emphasis mine).

That's it. That's what I want to write about in this book. The apostle Paul had very good reason for urging us to note these two seemingly opposite character traits—and it is a contrast that's been on my mind and heart for years now. It seems to me that our contemporary Christian culture has diminished, if not abandoned, biblical teaching about God's harsher attributes. An angry God doesn't sell well in our consumer-driven culture. But God is not an item on the shelf trying to appeal to our preferences.

We don't have to sell Him or market Him. He is who He is. Neither are God's attributes a box of chocolates; we can't pick or choose our favorite flavors.

Yes, *kindness* and *severity* seem poles apart. If we were evaluating people, we might find ourselves placing them in one pigeonhole or the other. Joe Smith is either kind or unkind. Jane Jones is either nice or nasty.

But what about God? How do we categorize the Almighty? One person makes a convincing case that He is very holy and severe in His judgments, while someone else characterizes Him as so loving and gracious He wouldn't deliberately hurt a fly. Maybe you have even heard someone say, "I love the Jesus of the New Testament, but I just can't relate with the angry God of the Old Testament." How could that be? He's the same God. We don't have two Gods, nor is Jesus an attempt to put a kinder face on the Father. To choose one deity—let's say, the kind one over the more severe one—is to create an *idol*. Something less than the God of Scripture.

Wherever I have ministered around the world, I have met professing Christians who worship a diminished God. The prosperity gospel sells well in less prosperous cultures because everybody wants a Jesus who loves us and desires us to be wealthy, healthy, and happy.

We don't have two Gods, nor is Jesus an attempt to put a kinder face on the Father.

Not everyone, however, chases after this kinder, gentler version of deity. I have also met Christians whose view of God has been warped and skewed by harsh religious legalism. In fact, I grew up with a few of them. They wear themselves out trying to keep rules and live with constant guilt and fear that God will punish them for any small infraction. Their view of God may be so unyielding and abrasive that they can't even relate to Him in a personal way. He is a strict Cosmic Cop who may or may not show up when we need Him, but we would never want Him as a next-door neighbor. Or a Father. Or a Friend.

In the pages that follow I will refer to the "older" and "newer" testaments. It was Dr. Ron Allen, one of my favorite professors at Western Seminary in Portland, Oregon, who first introduced me to the term "older testament." To speak of the *Old* Testament and *New* Testament may suggest that one is outdated and no longer relevant. On the door of my study I posted a sign that reads, "God spare me from two kinds of fools: One says, 'This is old, therefore it is good'; the other says, 'This is new, therefore it is better.'"[1]

Each morning I like to read a few comic strips from our local newspaper. Some offer profound insights about life. In a recent *Dennis the Menace* comic strip, Dennis and his parents have attended a church service and the pastor is standing at the door greeting his parishioners as they file out of the building. Dennis holds his little New Testament up to the preacher and says, "Did they havta buy the New Testament when the Old Testament wore out?" Perhaps Dennis reflects the opinion of many Christians today.

We have only one Bible, consisting of an older and a newer testament. Or, to describe it another way, we have one great library consisting of an older wing and a newer wing. Both wings of the library are filled with great literature, and we need the books in both wings to grasp the full story.

One big story runs throughout the entire Bible. Every book, whether long and challenging like Leviticus or short and sweet like Ruth, is part of the bigger story of redemption. Each author and each of the sixty-six books adds something irreplaceable to the story—and each helps us know God better.

We face no greater challenge in life than to know and to love God—the true God. In the preface of his book *The Pursuit of God,* A. W. Tozer spoke of being encouraged by a renewed thirst among some Christians to know God better. He wrote in

1948, "They are athirst for God, and they will not be satisfied till they have drunk deep at the Fountain of Living Water."[2]

Tozer, reaching back to the time of Elijah in 1 Kings 18:41–45, compared this renewed hunger for God with a "cloud the size of a man's hand."[3] I personally echo Tozer's passion for revival, but I question if he would still see that cloud the size of a man's hand today. In our rush to be popular, I fear the contemporary church may not even be looking up for a cloud.

There is but one true God, and He has revealed Himself as both severe in His holiness and gentle in His compassion. This is the God I will encourage us to consider in this book.

And that's my reason for writing a book that was never on my bucket list but happened anyway.

1

What Is God Like?

"What is God like?" How we answer that question is a matter of life and death, so we dare not get it wrong.

How can we comprehend a person who is invisible, transcendent, and infinite? If I can't even explain a solar eclipse to a three-year-old child, how can I, a finite creature, understand or comprehend God?

The short answer is, I can't.

Unless . . . *God reveals Himself to me.* Failing that, we are left to create God in any image we please. And that is precisely the problem. Someone once noted that God made us in His image, and ever since we have tried to do God a favor by making Him in *our* image. Sounds crazy? You bet, but that is what those who worship idols have done.

Psalm 50 portrays an angry God summoning Israel, His covenant people, into the courtroom. Fed up with their hypocrisy and injustice, He tells them: "These things you have done, and I have been silent; *you thought that I was one like yourself*" (Ps. 50:21, emphasis mine).

Timothy Keller describes modern thinking with these words: "Instead of trying to shape our desires to fit reality, we now seek to control and shape reality to fit our desires."[1] When we try to make God in our image, he (or she, or it, or they—you decide) becomes malevolent and capricious like us. To be malevolent is to be harsh, unkind, mean-spirited, or downright cruel. Capricious means fickle or unpredictable. A capricious person changes with the circumstances. Perhaps they had a bad night or got up on the wrong side of the bed, so everyone in the house or the office walks on eggshells to keep from "setting them off."

I regret the times my wife and sons had to deal with my capricious nature. I still wince when I think back to the day when Mary had to literally evacuate our sons from the house to spare them from my verbal anger. One of the older widows in our church had held me hostage on the phone for nearly half an hour trying to convince (compel, force, badger) me into changing our baptism service from Sunday evening to Sunday morning. Mrs. B (someday I hope to apologize to her in heaven) was absolutely relentless—the irresistible force. I tried to remain calm and strove to be reasonable, but my emotions began to rise within me like a volcano. If she was the irresistible force, then I was becoming the immovable object.

Sensing an impending eruption, Mary thought it prudent to take the boys shopping at a nearby department store. Truthfully, I pride myself for respecting widows and have done so through the years. But on that night, acting capriciously, I finally slammed the receiver down while Mrs. Bachar was still midsentence.

Hanging up on an elderly widow concerned about a baptism service. It wasn't my finest hour.

The God Who Does Not Grow Weary

One of the most painful memories of my youth occurred when I had just turned sixteen and had my shiny new driver's license. We were leaving for a vacation on the Poudre River in Colorado. I was driving and concentrating on keeping the car in the right lane on narrow old US Route 30. An oncoming semitruck was trying to pass

Our God works the night shift and the day shift, too, but He doesn't respond like that. He isn't capricious.

another truck but failing to make progress. Frankly, I didn't see it because I was concentrating on staying in my lane.

My sister warned me of the approaching problem so I could make necessary corrections, but my father suddenly lurched forward from the backseat and slugged me on the side of the head. A pastor by day and a police officer by night, he had just worked the night shift as a cop and was severely sleep deprived. At the church where he pastored, the sheep were being especially nasty, and Dad had been taking the brunt. As a result, I took the brunt of his frustration and weariness.

Our God works the night shift and the day shift, too, but He doesn't respond like that. He isn't capricious. He doesn't lash out in frustration, and He is never weary. Isaiah 40:28 described God this way, "Have you not known? Have you not heard? The LORD is the everlasting God, the Creator of the ends of the earth. He does not faint or grow weary; his understanding is unsearchable."

How about an example from the older testament? Elijah was a prophet during a very dark time in Israel's history. King Ahab had married Jezebel, the daughter of the king of Sidon and a worshiper of the pagan god Baal. Soon King Ahab began to worship Baal and even set up an image of Baal in Samaria. Suddenly Elijah appears on the scene to confront Ahab with a warning of severe drought. In the depths of the drought Elijah again confronts King Ahab and challenges him to a "throw down" on Mount Carmel. This was not an unknown chef challenging Bobby Flay on the Food Network but a challenge to see who could charbroil an entire beef carcass without a match—Yahweh or Baal?

Perhaps you remember how Elijah taunted the prophets of Baal on Mt. Carmel in 1 Kings 18? Perhaps Baal is sleeping! Perhaps he's using the toilet! In response to Elijah's taunting and Baal's silence, the false prophets became more zealous—even cutting themselves—as they attempted to rouse their wayward god. Still no one answered. All those frantic calls to Baal went to voicemail. He was nowhere to be found.

Compare Elijah's simple appeal to Yahweh, asking Him to send down fire from heaven to prove He is the one, true God. Fire from heaven ought to have been a simple task for Baal, the god of the storm.

In 1 Samuel 4, the Bible highlights a foolish attempt to manipulate God. Israel was still smarting from a shocking defeat at the hands of their perpetual nemesis, the powerful Philistine army. Incredulous that they, God's chosen, could have been defeated by a bunch of pagans, the Israelites decided to carry the ark of the covenant into battle the next day. With the ark present Israel was certain God would be compelled to fight for them.

> So the people sent to Shiloh and brought from there the ark of the covenant of the LORD of hosts, who is enthroned on the cherubim. And the two sons of Eli, Hophni and Phineas, were there with the ark of the covenant of God.
>
> As soon as the ark of the covenant of the LORD came into the camp [where it did not belong], all Israel gave a mighty shout, so that the earth resounded. (1 Sam. 4:4–5)

This may have been the first example of the "wave," popular at large sporting events a few years ago. With the ark of God leading the way, the Israelites had convinced themselves they couldn't lose.

But they did.

They were severely defeated once again, and the ark was captured by the Philistines. Hophni and Phineas, the evil sons of Israel's high priest, finally received the penalty they had deserved all along. At the news of their deaths, Eli collapsed and died on the spot. Phineas's pregnant wife died in childbirth, and the name she gave to her baby, Ichabod, says it all: "The glory of the LORD has departed." (How would you like *that* on your nametag?)

God simply cannot and will not be manipulated by our feeble, self-serving efforts. He is not capricious. He acts according to His true character. And on that dreadful day, His severity was on full display.

I witnessed the deep, elemental fear of offending pagan gods when I was teaching at a small Bible college in Uganda. Professing Christians make up the majority of the population, along with a sizable number of Muslims. But many Christians and Muslims who profess to be monotheistic continue to practice their traditional religions—including a form of ancestor worship.

God simply cannot and will not be manipulated by our feeble, self-serving efforts. He is not capricious.

The control these non-gods have over many Ugandans was evident in a small way on the campus of a small Bible college in Western Uganda where I taught. The wife of the college director died from complications in childbirth. The director eventually remarried a wonderful Christian woman. But when his wife began to experience significant physical symptoms, employees of the college became concerned that some people, perhaps even other Christians, would claim that an ancestor might be "paying the new wife back." Perhaps for marrying a man whose previous wife had died in childbirth. Who knows the reason? If it were true that an ancestor or some minor god was responsible for this good woman's physical symptoms, that would certainly be capricious.

As followers of Jesus, we know that God was not punishing the man or his wife, because our God is neither malevolent nor capricious. He is good. He is absolutely faithful in every situation.

The God Who Cannot Be Manipulated

While Mary, my wife, and I were on a combined pleasure and ministry trip to Ireland, I witnessed another example of how some people believe they can manipulate God. One afternoon we visited a site considered sacred to Roman Catholics. It was a small chapel perched on the top of an impressive mountain—with a fairly steep trail to the summit. Pilgrims from around the world climb this mountain in hope of receiving spiritual benefit. Below are the instructions printed on a large sign at the base of the mountain:

Croagh Patrick Pilgrimage

Every pilgrim who ascends the mountain on St. Patrick's Day or within the octave, or any time during the months of June, July, August & September & PRAYS IN OR NEAR THE CHAPEL for the intentions of our Holy Father the Pope, may gain a plenary indulgence on condition of going to Confession and Holy Communion on the Summit or within the week.

The sign explained three traditional stations on the summit

with instructions to fulfill all the requirements of each station. Note the instructions for the first station:

"The pilgrim walks seven times around the mountain saying seven Our Fathers, seven Hail Marys, and one Creed."

It might be easy for us to shake our heads and say, "How foolish. How useless." But maybe we who call ourselves Protestants need to evaluate our own practical faith system. Do we think similar thoughts?

How about the TV evangelist promising God will double any amount of money you donate to his/her television ministry? Or the pastor who assures us that the tithe offers God's guarantee to financial freedom?

Seems to me, the only difference is our motivation.

It is easy to slip into the mindset of expecting rewards from God when we do something good. I know because I've been there.

Several years ago, Open Doors Mission chose me to minister to the persecuted church in India. Accepting the invitation meant canceling a trip I had already scheduled to revisit our sister church in Latvia. Because I believed God had caused my name to be chosen, I accepted the call. Our church encouraged me to go and upheld me in prayer.

Boarding my flight in San Francisco to meet up with the rest of our team in Paris, I was disappointed when the man in the seat next to me suddenly began vomiting profusely as soon as we were in the air.

The rest of the red-eye flight was less than comfortable. I prayed not to catch whatever my seatmate had. After all, I was being faithful, so God should keep me safe. He owed me one, or so I thought. It didn't happen. I wasn't able to enjoy the wonderful Parisian café with my new teammates or the ride up the Eiffel Tower. My response, "God, after all I am doing for

You, why did You place me next to the one man on the plane who was ill?"

My Irish Catholic friends are seeking to receive mercy and escape pain in purgatory after they die, while my Protestant friends try to manipulate God so they can enjoy material prosperity and paradise here and now.

I'm reminded of the lyrics from the song "Something Good" in the musical *The Sound of Music*. Julie Andrews, in the role of Maria, was dancing with Captain von Trapp. Amazed the captain had fallen in love with her, Maria assumes somewhere in her past she must have done something very good to deserve his love.[2]

I love the song, but the thought certainly isn't biblical. It resembles the Buddhist concept of karma. Even so, we all fall into this sort of thinking from time to time. We assume if we do something really good—like sharing the gospel with a stranger or taking care of a sick neighbor—that we'll gain points with God, and some extra blessing. *Christianity Today* includes the following statistics from a Lifeway Research survey of Evangelicals who attend a Protestant church monthly or more: 75% agree that "God wants me to prosper financially"; 41% agree their church "teaches that if I give more money to my church and charities God will bless me in return"; 26% agree that "to receive material blessings from God, I have to do something for God."[3]

Again, it isn't true. God can't be manipulated. He isn't Santa Claus, and He doesn't have angels keeping track of who is naughty and who is nice. Well then, if He's not like these caricatures, what *is* He like?

Here's where we get some really good news. Our wonderful, awesome, holy, and incomprehensible God has chosen to *reveal* Himself to you and me!

Psalm 19 declares God has shown Himself through the

natural world and through Scripture. (Pause for a minute or two and read Psalm 19.) The first six verses invite us to look up and listen as "The heavens declare the glory of God." David describes God's revelation in nature by using terms related to audible sounds such as voice, proclaim, speech, and words. It is as if God is speaking to us through His Creation wherever we are, anytime, day or night.

I recently taught a class on the Psalms and used Psalm 19 to demonstrate that God speaks through creation and His written Word. I suggested a title for a sermon from Psalm 19: "Can you hear me now?" Perhaps you recall a TV commercial from a cellular phone company using that question several years ago.[4] God continues to speak to us through His Word and His creation. The question remains, are we listening?

We have yet to discover the borders of this expansive universe that is like an artist's canvas displaying God's handiwork 24/7. His limitless creativity and love for beauty is on display in every sunrise and sunset.

Have you ever visited the Hubble Telescope website? Whenever I visit the site, I am amazed at the pictures taken from the Hubble Telescope while it is exploring outer space and sending back pictures of galaxies and supernovas. On a recent visit to Hubblesite.org, I was in awe of the multiwavelength pictures of the Crab Nebula and Spiral Galaxy Pair NGC4302. My response was to wonder why God created a universe so expansive and filled with such indescribable beauty. The answer? He is displaying His glory and His power. The universe is His art gallery, and I am invited to stroll breathlessly through it. Hubble brings many of the works of God's mouth-gaping art up close.

The universe is so unbelievably intricate that astronomers could predict the precise time, 10:19 a.m., when the total solar eclipse would arrive near our hometown of Bend, Oregon, on August 21, 2017. To the second, they predicted how long "totality" would last at any given point along the journey of the solar eclipse from the west coast to the eastern seaboard.

Psalm 19 also declares this universe of ours didn't happen by chance in some random and incomprehensible "big bang." In fact, it is the personal handiwork of God. The computer I am using at this very moment didn't just happen when chemical particles bumped into each other. It is the product of intelligent and skilled people. Paul concluded the same of creation in Romans 1:18–20 and boldly declared that nobody can say "I had no idea God exists" because the evidence is all around us.

The God Who Wrote Us a Love Letter

We can only learn so much about God from studying creation. We see His infinite power and His glory displayed everywhere we look. We see His love for beauty. But how could we learn about His character? How could we know for certain God is love? Or that He is holy, patient, or even severe? I need a clearer disclosure. God has provided that in His Word, the Bible.

In Psalm 19:7, David turns his attention to the Scriptures, God's written revelation of Himself. In the days before Scripture was complete, God also revealed Himself to people through visions, dreams, and theophanies—appearances of God in visible form. Sometimes the second person of the Trinity appeared in human form to Abraham and other people in Genesis 12, 15, 22 and other passages.

In Joshua 5:13–15, Joshua prepared to lead the army of Israel against Jericho. He was near Jericho when he looked up and saw a man standing in front of him with drawn sword in his hand. The moment was filled with emotions of fear and uncertainty. Wouldn't you feel a tad bit of fear? Joshua challenged the apparent intruder, saying in effect, "Are you friend or foe?"

The warrior's reply was startling. "No, but I am the commander of the army of the LORD." This was the pre-incarnate Christ claiming He was the "five-star" general who would lead the army to victory.

What was Joshua's response when he met God on the shores of the Jordan River? He "fell on his face to the earth and worshiped."

The Lord of the Army continued, "Take off your sandals from your feet, for the place where you are standing is holy." Joshua made haste to obey. Doesn't this remind us of the burning bush experience of Moses when he first met the living God?

Joshua learned that God is holy and will not be trivialized. I wonder, are we in danger of forgetting that fact? Has the pendulum swung so far in favor of God's kindness and grace that we have diminished or ignored His holiness and severity?

God has revealed Himself up close and personal through His Son, Jesus of Nazareth. He is the perfect reflection of God.

Finally, God has also revealed Himself to us in the person of Jesus Christ as recorded in Hebrews 1:1–4.

> Long ago, at many times and in many ways, God spoke to our fathers by the prophets, but in these last days he has spoken to us by his Son, whom he appointed the heir of all things, through whom also he created the world. He is the radiance of the glory of God and the exact imprint of his nature, and he upholds the universe by the word of his power. After making purification for sins, he sat down

at the right hand of the Majesty on high, having become as much superior to angels as the name he has inherited is more excellent than theirs.

God has revealed Himself up close and personal through His Son, Jesus of Nazareth. He is the perfect reflection of God. Consider Jesus' own words: "If you knew me, you would know my Father also. . . . I and the Father are one" (John 8:19; 10:30).

So let us praise our Creator God who chose not to remain shrouded in mystery but reveals Himself to us as a kind, loving, merciful, and forgiving God. But let's not forget God is also holy and severe, as demonstrated in the death of Christ on the cross.

Here is what I like to think about: when I really want to know what my God and Creator is truly like, all I have to do is stop and consider Jesus of Nazareth. Was there ever a more loving person? Was there ever a more powerful person, One who could calm the storm and heal the leper? Was there ever a kinder person, someone who took time in His demanding schedule to cuddle little children? Was there ever a more giving person, One who gave the ultimate gift—His own life? And was there ever a more severe person than the Galilean driving moneychangers out of the temple and calling religious leaders snakes and whitewashed tombs?

No other person has ever lived this life with kindness and severity or grace and truth in perfect balance.

And no one ever will.

Personally, I want to know Him and to experience His presence and His power in my life. How about you? If that desire also describes you, let's continue the journey together.

2

First Impressions

"Good morning, Preach."

I looked up at the man approaching me on the trail. I didn't know him, but he evidently knew me.

Preach? That particular greeting could only mean one thing. "So you've been hanging around Ed Neff," I said with a smile. Ed was the only person on the planet who called me Preach.

We stopped for a moment on the path descending the summit of Pilot Butte, a five-hundred-foot volcanic cinder cone here in Bend, Oregon. It's a vigorous but relatively easy climb on a dusty trail traversed by scores of hikers every day. And no wonder. From the summit, the panoramic view of the Cascade mountains west of the city is truly spectacular.

My first impressions of Troll, the man who had greeted me on the trail, were mixed. He wore shorts and had shoulder-length hair confined in a ponytail. His mustache covered his lips and drooped over the sides of his mouth. And to be honest, it seemed just a tad brash for someone to call a total stranger "Preach."

As it turned out, my old friend Ed Neff had been best pals with Troll in California. They had recently been reunited in Bend. Ed invited Troll and his wife, Sharran, to visit First Baptist Church . . . where Troll heard me give the message.

After chatting a few minutes on the trail, we said a congenial goodbye and went on our way. I began watching for Troll and Sharran on Sunday mornings so I could visit with them before the service began.

Before long, Troll and I began meeting on the summit of the butte early in the morning so we could descend together. A friendship blossomed, and we began to meet in the parking lot to do the whole hike together. Now, seven years later, we drive out of town to climb Bessie Butte. We've also taken several trips exploring central and eastern Oregon.

Troll and I agree that never have two more unlikely guys become "hiking buddies." I'm a blue jeans man; Troll wears shorts or sweat pants. My hair is fairly short and I visit my barber regularly. Troll claims he can't pronounce the word *barber*, so his ponytail is safe. My life has been squeaky clean, at least on the surface. Troll, on the other hand, has experimented with drugs and illicit sex. I grew up with a mother and father who loved my sister and me. Troll's father was an abusive alcoholic who deserted his family when Troll was around seven years old, leaving a little boy to be raised by a single mother. As I write, I have been married more than fifty-two years to my wife, Mary. Troll deserted his wife and twin daughters when they were still young. In my Nebraska childhood church, Troll would have been pigeonholed as a "pagan" and, sadly, not been welcomed.

Regardless of how different our lives have been, today we are brothers in Christ and best friends. After Troll became a follower of Jesus, his life changed dramatically. Thirty-eight years after deserting his wife and daughters, Troll returned to Bend to apologize to them—an act that must have taken immense courage. Only the grace of God could have reconciled Troll and Sharran, but they are once again husband and wife. She now has advanced dementia and lives in a memory care facility for her own safety. Troll visits her every day. His love and commitment to Sharran, who no longer remembers his name, amazes me.

Troll would say I have had a significant impact on his life and faith, but the influence has been mutual. Through the years, I have been moved and inspired by observing my friend's simple, yet deep, faith. We never climb together without Troll standing on the summit raising his hands toward the rising sun or the Cascades proclaiming, "This is the day the Lord has made, let us rejoice and be glad in it! It's all about You, Jesus, and the Holy Spirit who dwells within. Amen."

Typically, he will then turn to me and say, "I love you, Preach." Actually, we say it in unison. I can't count how many times that has happened, but it still moves me.

Troll was not his birth name. What mother would wish that on her son? But Troll assures me that Larry, the name on his birth certificate, was not someone worth remembering. God's grace is making him into a new person in the image of Jesus.

My experience with Troll reminds me that first impressions are not always accurate. This is especially true when it comes to our perceptions of God.

The Cosmic Cop

Family, culture, religious training, and life experiences all influence our perception of God.

How would being raised Hindu have influenced my view of the divine? How would Islam or the Quran have shaped my view of Allah? How would growing up in a Native American culture influence my impressions about the Great Spirit? How would I view God if I had grown up in a very strict, legalistic church?

Well, that last question isn't hypothetical. I was raised in a strict, legalistic, conservative Christian family and church, and it provided me with a long list of forbidden activities. *Real* Christians didn't smoke or chew tobacco. They didn't drink alcohol, either, because Jesus drank grape juice, not real wine. (Or so they told me.) We also didn't approve of dancing or going to the movies.

To be fair, I am grateful for the strict teaching that helped keep me from making harmful choices. I've never had to struggle with chemical addictions like my best friend in high school, who died from alcoholism. My church also taught me a respect for the Bible, and verses that I memorized in Sunday school became valuable resources as a young man. When I attended Moody Bible Institute, I was already familiar with the Scriptures. In youth group, I often won the "sword drill" competition to see who could find a biblical passage first.

I'm confident that words like "love" and "grace" came up in the Sunday sermons and in our conversations, but a strong emphasis on performance and rule-keeping overshadowed everything else. We may have called God "Father," but I grew up with the distinct impression that His real job was policeman, a stern and keen-eyed Cosmic Cop. It didn't help that my father was uniquely bi-vocational—a preacher at the fundamental Baptist church by day and a police officer by night.

Being a preacher's kid gave my sister and me even more rules to keep. Both of us were compliant, and we learned to perform in order to please our parents and impress the watching church members. (And count on it, they were *always* watching.)

We got along. But it wasn't much fun.

All those manmade rules robbed me of joy. In my mind, God was the great spoiler, making certain I couldn't have fun like my friends. He was the Eye-in-the-Sky, always spying on me (usually frowning in disapproval).

In Sunday school we learned a song that went like this: "Oh be careful little hands what you do . . . Oh be careful little eyes what you see . . . Oh be careful little mouth what you say, for *the Father up above is looking down in love . . ."*[1]

I realize the song was meant to teach that God is big and powerful and knows everything. But to my ears, the lyrics came across more like an ultimatum. I had better be very good because God was up there observing my every move and recording everything I said or did—so that He could punish me when I stepped out of line. Somehow I missed those words, "looking down in love." It felt more like that old threat, "Wait till your father gets home." Only in this case I wasn't just dreading my dad's return. It was *God*!

> It felt more like that old threat, "Wait till your father gets home." Only in this case I wasn't just dreading my dad's return. It was *God*!

The lyrics of the song came back to haunt me in my teens. I had invited a girl on a date to see a movie at a drive-in theater. (Do you remember those?) Of course I dared not go to The Plains Drive-in Theater in my hometown because someone might see us. (Informants were everywhere.) So we drove to Kimball, forty-five miles west on Route 30. As I approached the theater, I was bursting with the anticipation of eating forbidden fruit. Nobody would ever know. But naive as I was, I entered the exit, bypassing the ticket counter. As a result, an angry proprietor came running with his flashlight to interrogate me in front of my date.

Busted! Immediately I knew the Cosmic Cop had caught me. In the very act.

A Stern, Indifferent God

How would it have been different if I had been raised in a Muslim family?

While we were students at Moody Bible Institute, my wife, Mary, and I considered becoming missionaries to Muslims, so I tried to learn what I could about Islam. A Muslim must recite the *Shahada:* "There is no God but Allah, and Muhammad is the messenger of Allah." Prayers are also recited five times daily while facing Mecca. Devout Muslims are to do charity, fast, and—if they can possibly afford it—make a pilgrimage to Mecca at least once in their lives.

Nabeel Qureshi knew what it is like to be reared in a Muslim home. He is the author of the book *No God but One: Allah or Jesus?* Responding to the question of whether Allah is the same as the God of the Bible, Nabeel shares several insights. First, he points out that while the God of the Bible is triune, Allah is monad—only one. Allah judges sin by the scale method; a few smaller sins are nothing to worry about. The real God of the Bible, of course, views sin differently. All sin is serious and worthy of death or separation from God. The God of the Bible has revealed Himself to us and desires a relationship with us—even to the point of pursuing us in an effort to reconcile us to Himself. Allah, on the other hand, has no interest in seeking a relationship with people.

"Truly," Nabeel writes, "nothing else in the Quran appears to indicate that Allah wants a relationship with humans. This is especially true of a father-child relationship, as the Quran specifically denies that Allah is a father. . . . . When Jews and Christians suggest they are children of God, the Quran says to castigate them."[2]

In the same chapter, Nabeel writes, "Allah intends man to pursue the relationship of a servant to his master, but *not the relationship of a child with his father.* Nothing in

> "Nothing in the Quran suggests that Allah desires intimacy with humanity. We are not his beloved— just one of his creatures."

the Quran suggests that Allah desires intimacy with humanity. We are not his beloved—just one of his creatures."[3]

If we had been raised in a Muslim household, then, our view of God would be someone to please and serve dutifully— not someone to love and know intimately. No matter what you hear from Muslim communicators on the evening news, many atrocities being committed in the name of Allah can be justified through the Quran. The contrast between Muhammad and Jesus Christ, who said to turn the other cheek and love your enemy, could not be starker. Muhammad, the prophet of Allah, advocated violence. Compare that with Jesus who said to turn the other cheek and do good to your enemies. (Luke 6:27–31)

Multiple Impressions

In stark contrast to the harshness of Islam, if I had been raised in a very permissive, secular family, I might view God as a doting grandfather. No matter how badly I behaved, He would always smile, shake His head, and say with a sigh, "Oh well, it can't be helped. Boys will be boys." Some who claim to be Christians worship this kind of God. They believe God is too kind to punish anybody by sending them to hell, that He always forgives everybody whether they seek forgiveness or not.

As a nineteenth-century German writer said on his deathbed, "Of course God will forgive me. That's His job."[4]

Is it possible that those who have perverted the genuine gospel of Jesus Christ with a cross-less social gospel or the prosperity gospel are worshiping a false god who must forgive us because it's His job? Are they ignoring God's holiness and severity while pursuing a weak kind of granddaddy deity who will just let "boys be boys"? That God may feel good (until you really need Him), but He is neither righteous nor just. God's severity is the outworking of His holiness.

In contrast, pantheism is the belief that everything in the universe, both animate and inanimate, is God. For those who have chosen this path, God is not a person but rather some force or energy. God may be Mother Nature or the Great Spirit that lives in everything around us. This is the god behind the Star Wars movies, with its repeated mantra: "May the force be with you." Today we may associate this with New Age religion or with dualism—the belief that both God and the universe have existed eternally. Thus there are two ultimate forces in the universe, God and matter, resulting in a conflict between God and evil aspects in the material universe. The Force has both a good and an evil side.

Two words contrast the biblical God with that of pantheism and New Age philosophy: *immanent* and *transcendent*.

To be immanent in the pantheistic sense is to indwell or be inherent within something. The god of pantheism is intrinsic or a natural part of creation rather than the Creator who is separate from creation. He is in the tree or cow or moon or stars. This deity may be "all around us" but we can't relate to him personally. How could we? He isn't a person at all. However, the Bible teaches that God *is* immanent or omnipresent (present everywhere). God is near to us and also personal enough to relate to us.

Transcendence, however, means that God—the *real* God—is outside this world. Not only is He outside of or distinct from what He has created, He is also not governed by anything He has created. He transcends, or rises above, creation. He is infinite and boundless, distinct from what His hands have formed. And even though this Creator dwells outside of His handiwork, He is *personal* and relates with His creation. In other words, God has come near to us in the person of Jesus Christ—Immanuel. God is a person—Father, Son, and Holy Spirit—and He is relational.

Several years ago, Open Doors Mission invited me to minister to the persecuted church in India. As the days went by, I saw how Hinduism has affected every part of that culture. Having observed Hindu shrines, I witnessed no image that communicated love or anything desirable.

If I had been raised in a polytheistic religion such as Hinduism, animism, or other traditional indigenous religions, my gods would be unpredictable, malevolent, or mean-spirited.

The 1980 movie *The Gods Must Be Crazy* illustrates this point with ironic humor. At one time, missionary candidates with WorldVenture watched this movie as part of their cross-cultural training. The movie tells the story of Xi, a bushman from the San people inhabiting the Kalahari Desert. A Coke bottle tossed from an airplane landed unbroken on the soft desert sand. Since it fell from the sky, Xi's people assumed it must be a gift from the gods. As time went on, the bush people discovered many valuable uses for the bottle, and in the process created a great demand for it. But since there was only one Coke bottle, conflict over who could use it became severe, disrupting the tribe's tranquility.

The village elders finally agreed that it had to be returned to the gods, and Xi was assigned to carry the bottle "to the end of the world" and throw it away.

The movie may be charming and funny, but real-life polytheism and animism are neither. The malevolent gods or spirits control the lives of their worshipers/victims, who live in constant fear they may offend these unpredictable supernatural powers. The Bible portrays an idol as worthless, dead, blind, and deaf. Adherence to such false deities could, however, be deadly—and in some instances included the cruel sacrifice of children and even little babies. Leviticus 18:21 describes the god Molech as detestable because he demanded his worshipers to throw their children into the fire to please him.

These gods, like their creators, were limited in their power and authority. One god might rule during the springtime but surrender to another god in the summer. Other gods ruled in mountainous areas but were weak in the valleys. In 1 Kings 20:23–30, the armies of Israel under King Ahab soundly defeated a stronger Syrian army in the hill country of Samaria. Following that military disaster, advisors to Syria's King Benhadad claimed they had it all figured out. "Their gods," the advisors explained, "are the gods of the hills, and so they were stronger than we. But let them fight us on the plain, and surely we shall be stronger than they." But the true God is God of the valleys as well. Not only were 100,000 Syrians killed in battle with Israel, but God pushed over a wall onto tens of thousands more!

In my daily reading through the Psalms, I was recently reminded that Yahweh is not limited by geography or circumstances. Psalm 29 describes Yahweh's sovereign rule in the heavens above and in the seas. He rules over the mountains, breaks the great cedars of Lebanon, and causes Mount Hermon to skip like a young wild ox.

Wherever the light of the gospel penetrates the darkness and superstition of a polytheistic culture, people are released from their dread and fear of the spirits after they fall in love with Jesus.

I'm not sure what a skipping mountain would actually look like, but the underlying point is clear. God rules over the storm and in the forests. He is enthroned everywhere and over everything. Period. End of discussion.

Wherever the light of the gospel penetrates the darkness and superstition of a polytheistic culture, people are released from their dread and fear of the spirits after they fall in love with Jesus. Missionary books such as *Through Gates of Splendor* or *Peace Child* are testimonies to the power of the gospel to transform an entire culture and are well worth reading if you haven't had the chance.

Disappointment and Doubt

Culture and religion aren't the only experiences that shape our view of the Almighty. Our perspective of God may also be influenced by devastating experiences in life, such as the death of a child or spouse or the loss of a home to fire or a tornado. Isn't it interesting that we call these events "acts of God"? When bad things happen to kind people, we may accuse God of being an absent landlord because He seems so disinterested, negligent, and unfair.

Many of us have been taught that the God we worship is omnipotent (all powerful) and sovereign (rules over everything). When traumatic circumstances crash into our lives, however, the very truths that once encouraged us now plague us with questions. We might summarize our struggle something like this: "Either God is good but not all powerful, or He is powerful but not good."

Asaph, a composer of several psalms, described a time when he almost jettisoned his faith when he struggled over the injustices and inequities he had experienced in his life. "But as for me, my feet had almost stumbled, my steps had nearly slipped. For I was envious of the arrogant when I saw the prosperity of the wicked" (Ps. 73:2–3). Another translation puts it like this: "I almost lost my footing. My feet were slipping, and

I was almost gone" (NLT). But when Asaph looked at his situation again through the eyes of faith, he realized the story wasn't over. Not by a long shot.

When life seems unfair, disappointment may become doubt. Some people may even turn away from their faith because God has not lived up to their expectations. One of the most dramatic examples is Charles Templeton, who once professed to be a Christian and even became the pastor of a conservative church in Canada. Templeton was instrumental in the establishment of Youth for Christ with his friend Billy Graham.

Popular author Lee Strobel shares the story of Templeton's struggle with the presence of so much pain and suffering in the world. If God was all powerful, kind, and good, then how in the world could He *allow* such terrible suffering in the lives of so many people? Templeton stumbled hard over that seeming contradiction, and eventually renounced his faith, declaring himself to be an agnostic.[5]

What do we make of the atheist who refuses to believe in any god?

First, some atheists believe that there is no God based upon the worldview in which they were raised or trained. In my opinion, their choice to deny God in spite of the evidence is the result of flawed thinking. That is not to say atheists are all stupid. They have simply made choices resulting in their conclusions.

> **Without God in the equation we are free to live life as we please, without fear of consequences or ultimate accountability.**

Second, I suspect that some who deny the existence of God do so for emotional reasons rather than from a lack of evidence. Without God in the equation we are free to live as we please, without fear of consequences or ultimate accountability. Others have looked at the evidence and have failed to find it convincing. Those who choose to reject Him can always find an excuse against the evidence they do have. But that's not to say skeptics and atheists are bad people who don't do altruistic acts.

In his book *The Rage Against God*, Peter Hitchens shares his personal story of casting off his childhood religion. "There were no more external, absolute rules. . . . I did not have to do anything that I did not want to do, ever again. I would therefore be 'happy,' because I was freed from those things whereof my conscience was afraid. . . . I could behave as I wished, without fear of eternal consequences."[6]

Hitchens wonders why atheists do not rejoice in their lack of absolute moral standards and adds, "Might it be because they fear that, by admitting their delight at the non-existence of good and evil, they are revealing something of their motives for their belief? Could it be that the last thing on earth they wish to acknowledge is that they have motives for their belief . . . ?"[7] Hitchens quotes Thomas Nagel, "It isn't just that I don't believe in God and, naturally, hope that I'm right in my belief. It's that I hope there is no God! I don't want there to be a God."[8]

This is the same point Paul makes in Romans 1:18–32. It is not a lack of evidence but a deliberate choice to ignore the evidence that is all around us all the time.

Life and Death

It is encouraging to read the stories of believers who have faced suffering and injustice, but have refused to blame God or become bitter. Perhaps the most graphic example in Scripture is Joseph. His confidence in God matured through long seasons of suffering. Eventually he could face the very brothers who had sold him into slavery and declare, "You meant evil against me, but God meant it for good" (Gen. 50:20). God used Joseph's painful experiences to spare the nation Israel through a severe famine and preserve the promised seed.

I watched my parents work through the tragic death of my eight-year-old brother. Danny's life was literally ripped from him by an intoxicated driver on the gravel road in front of our farmhouse. Mom and Dad had only been Christ followers for a year or so when that tragedy overshadowed our family. No parent expects to bury his or her child. Although I can't speak from personal experience, I suspect that it must be like having your heart ripped out of your chest. Church members encouraged my father to sue the farmer who had provided the alcohol to minors. Instead, Dad quoted Romans 12:19: "Vengeance is mine, I will repay, saith the Lord" (KJV).

My mother, although very young in the faith, could still sing with her deep alto voice:

God hath not promised skies always blue,
Flower-strewn pathways all our lives through
God hath not promised sun without rain,
Joy without sorrow, peace without pain.
But God hath promised strength for the day,
Rest for the labor, light for the way,
Grace for the trials, help from above,
Unfailing sympathy, undying love.[9]

Just minutes ago, when I went to the internet to double-check the lyrics to this song that Mother used to sing, I was caught by surprise. I had expected to find printed lyrics, which I did. But I was blindsided by the clear sound of a piano playing the melody. Out of nowhere, tears streamed down my face.

It was like a dam burst. Just for an instant, I could have sworn it was Mom playing the piano, with me sitting beside her on the piano bench as we used to do. "*Strength for the day . . . rest for the labor . . . light for the way.*"

As a pastor, I've been at the bedside of a number of dying people, believers and unbelievers alike. The difference between them couldn't be starker, not only for the person who passes, but for those who remain behind. In 1 Thessalonians 4:13, Paul encourages believers whose loved ones had died, "But we do not want you to be uninformed, brothers, about those who are asleep, *that you may not grieve as others do who have no hope*" (emphasis mine).

In the verses that follow the passage above, Paul concludes with a reminder that we will be reunited with our loved ones to spend eternity in the presence of Christ. An atheist has no such prospect. Those who reject God in this life may find themselves with a great measure of success, prosperity, respect, and fame. But what they don't have is hope beyond the grave. And that's the one thing a dying person wants most.

On July 10, 2015, my father took his final breath here in Bend while I was holding his hand. One moment Dad was there with me in the room; the next moment he was in the presence of his Lord and Savior. I said goodbye with warm tears washing my face but with the deepest assurance that I will see my father again. Yes, I felt grief, but hope was already flooding through my soul. Why? Because I believe in the God who revealed Himself to us in the person of Jesus Christ, the very One who wrestled our final enemy, Death, to the mat and won!

The greatest challenge you and I will face in our lifetime is to gain an accurate perspective of the living God. *Everything* else depends on this. Happily, that doesn't mean we have to search every corner of the earth or scan the universe to obtain such knowledge. That's because God has most carefully, clearly, and lovingly shown Himself to people like you and me.

In the following chapter, we will meet a man who met God up close and personal, and his perception of God underwent a drastic change. We will meet a man who experienced God, and whose thirst was forever quenched. We will also meet the God who offers you and me living water.

3

From Prince of Egypt to Friend of God

The LORD would speak to Moses face to face,
as one speaks to a friend.

Exodus 33:11 NLT

"Out of the ordinary . . . Out of this world."

Just now, those phrases caught my eye as I scanned Hub-bleSite, the official website for the Hubble Telescope. "Outside this world" are the words I used to describe God's transcendence in the last chapter.

Prior to 1610, when Galileo turned his telescope toward the heavens, what we could see with the naked eye was all we knew of our vast star field. (Even so, try to imagine looking up at the Milky Way in a world without a single electric light. That must have been pretty spectacular in itself.) Galileo and his telescope introduced the world to even more marvels, opening "the final frontier," as they used to say on Star Trek.

When the Hubble Space Telescope was launched on April 24, 1990, our knowledge of the universe suddenly, exponentially, expanded. Jaw-dropping photographs of supernovas, spiral galaxies, and never-seen-before phenomena have since been routinely beamed back to earth, exploding our knowledge of the heavens. The Hubble website frequently releases new images from deep outer space. Whether we are hard-core science fiction fans or career astrophysicists, we can only imagine the wonders that might await us if we could somehow explore the nameless planets and multiplied stellar splendors of that distant island universe.

Tranquilly orbiting 340 miles above the earth, Hubble peers into deep space—and possibly the roots of time itself. No matter how much we discover about the universe, no matter how this body of knowledge grows, there will always be more that remains hidden.

That is also true about God.

Yet even though God is so great, so mind-bendingly awesome, and so transcendent that words can never fully describe Him, He has not left us to grope blindly in our search to know Him. Thankfully, God has chosen to reveal Himself to people like you and me.

Let's consider the experience of a man whose first impressions were dramatically altered after several highly personal encounters with the living, eternal God.

An Encounter that Changes Everything

The life of Moses divides neatly into three segments of approximately forty years each. Moses was the third child of Hebrew slaves in Egypt. His devout father and mother had only a few short years to indoctrinate their son in the faith of their forefathers. The living God had appeared to Abraham, Isaac, and Jacob. All who followed stood on the shoulders of these men.

In Exodus 2, we read that Moses had already been condemned to death by Pharaoh's decree that every male Hebrew baby was to be tossed into the Nile as crocodile food. I believe Jochebed, Moses's mother, hid her baby where he would most likely be rescued by Pharaoh's daughter. Jochebed hoped the princess would feel compassion for the little one, and that's exactly what happened. In God's matchless providence, the royal daughter of Pharaoh chose to adopt the baby—and even hired Jochebed to nurse Moses.

We don't know how much time Jochebed had to plant seeds of faith in Moses, but she redeemed every moment. Eventually the heartbreaking day arrived when Moses became the grandson of Pharaoh and royal Egyptian prince. He was educated in the ways of Egypt and was also introduced to the pantheon of Egyptian gods. Moses was an Egyptian in dress and custom and participated in pagan religious observances. It would have been natural for him to embrace the polytheism of his peers and view his world through the lens of idolatry.

And perhaps he did, for a time. But Moses never forgot his roots.

Somewhere in the deepest crevices of his Egyptian soul there remained the seed of a son of Abraham.

One day he observed the miserable conditions of his biological people, the Hebrews. Somewhere in the deepest crevices of his Egyptian soul there remained the seed of a son of Abraham. His passion for justice resulted in the death of an Egyptian and Moses's need to escape the wrath of Pharaoh.[1]

For the next forty years, Moses lived the life of a nomadic shepherd. The hustle and bustle of the royal courts must have seemed like a distant dream. The banquets, the honors, the ceremonies, the personal chariot, the fear and esteem of multitudes . . . it was all a million miles away. Now he slept on the ground under the stars, listening to the small night sounds of desert creatures and the stirrings of a restless sheep. Moses was in the school of solitude, and the Bible never tells us whether he liked it or not. He married the daughter of a Midianite priest. His skin became dark and weathered under the blazing sun and the desert wind. Perhaps this once-royal prince felt like his life had lost purpose and meaning.

By contrast, life as a shepherd must have been mundane, to say the least. The scenery seldom changed, and the routine was the same: lead the flock to water and grass, let them rest and chew the cud, and gather them at night. Then rise early the next morning and repeat the cycle. Dealing with occasional wilderness predators must have seemed like a welcome diversion.

But then . . . one ordinary day suddenly turned extraordinary when "the angel of the LORD appeared to him in a flame of fire out of the midst of a bush. He looked, and behold, the bush was burning, yet it was not consumed" (Ex. 3:2).

This was like no fire Moses had ever seen. How strange! The bush was in flames, but nothing changed, nothing burned up. Could he possibly have seen green, unsinged leaves through the flames? Then the angel of the LORD revealed Himself to Moses from the bush. "The angel of the LORD" is usually a reference to the second person of the Trinity, whom we now know as Jesus Christ.

Moses was witnessing a *theophany*, an appearance of God in a visible form. The almighty Creator of the universe was introducing Himself to a has-been shepherd on the backside of Midian.

Scripture says, "When *the LORD* saw that he turned aside to see, *God called to him* out of the bush, 'Moses, Moses!' And he said, 'Here I am'" (Ex. 3:3–4, emphasis mine).

Note two names in the above sentence: The LORD and

God. "Lord" is the Hebrew word Yahweh, the name God uses when He reveals Himself to people or enters into a covenant with them. The word "God" or "Elohim" suggests God's might and power.

Now—just for a moment and as best we can—let's put ourselves into Moses's sandals. An inexplicable phenomenon has drawn each of us to a bush, filling us with wonder and curiosity. Suddenly a voice reverberates from the bush and calls us by name! Curiosity morphs into fear as the voice warns, "*Do not come near; take your sandals off your feet, for the place on which you are standing is holy ground*" (Ex. 3:5, emphasis mine).

I don't know how you would feel, but goose bumps are racing up and down my spine. My sandals are off and my legs have turned to Jell-O. I fear for my life. God continues, "I am the God of your father, the God of Abraham, the God of Isaac, and the God of Jacob." Names spoken by his Hebrew mother echo back from distant memory. Afraid to look at God, Moses covers his face.

Standing barefoot near the bush, unnerved and trembling with fear, what are Moses's first impressions of God? If this was the only time God appeared to Moses, how would he describe the encounter? What would he say about this meeting with his Creator? What would *you* say?

If I were Moses, I would conclude that He is holy and won't be treated with disrespect. I would have kicked off my shoes and covered my face right along with Moses. From that encounter, I would realize that God is powerful, supernatural, and mysterious, because nobody has ever set fire to a bush without turning it to ash.

But I would also know for sure that God is a person who knows me by name.

And that fact alone would blow my mind.

God continues to peel back the shroud of secrecy with Moses when He tells him that He had seen the afflictions of His people struggling under bondage and had also heard their cry for help. In other words, God cares about His people. He is neither absent nor capricious. God continues, "I know their sufferings, and I have come down to deliver them out of the hand of the Egyptians and to bring them up out of that land to a good and broad land, a land flowing with milk and honey" (Ex. 3:7–8).

In that moment, Moses learns that God is compassionate and kind to victims of oppression. He is not only transcendent, out of this world, but He condescends to be involved with us in the pits of life.

God tells Moses to return to Egypt, promising to be with him and to meet him and the people of Israel on the mountain near the flaming bush. Then He shares His name with the elderly shepherd, saying, "I AM WHO I AM" (Ex. 3:14). In other words, I am the eternal One. I am self-sufficient; I lack nothing and need nothing, for I am everything you will ever need and so much more.

After forty years of obscurity and isolation, Moses had very little confidence. How could he possibly accomplish the daring exploits God seemed to be calling him to do? In response, the Lord offers physical evidence to prove He will keep His promises. The shepherd's staff becomes a snake—the inanimate becomes animate! A moment later, Moses's hand suddenly turns "leprous like snow." Then God restores it to normal (Ex. 4:1–9). Moses's impression about God is growing and changing by the moment. He discovers that the God his mother had taught him about so many years ago is the living God, the Creator. He is holy and demands to be treated respectfully. But He is also kind and compassionate! Moses's relationship with God deepens.

With God's promises and the vivid memory of the burning bush fixed in his mind, Moses is at last confident that returning to Egypt is his true calling in life. He receives permission from his father-in-law to return to Egypt with his wife and sons—who were probably ready to leave Midian for an extended road trip. Conversation returns to the burning bush as the boys ask their dad to tell the story again and again.

All too soon, however, Moses will be reminded that God, although kind and compassionate, is also holy and will not be trivialized. Camping at the local KOA, everyone in the family is sleeping contentedly when suddenly "the Lord met him and sought to put him to death" (Ex. 4:24).

I don't understand all that happened on that strange, terrifying night, except that Zipporah, Moses's Midianite wife, apparently had to put on a surgeon's gown and circumcise her sons in order to stay the hand of God upon her husband. Moses had neglected to carry out the sign of the covenant God had made with Abraham. If Moses was to deliver the Hebrew people, he must first honor the God of the covenant. Neglecting this central point had put his life at risk.

After that traumatic experience, Moses sends his family back home and travels alone. Without the conversation of wife and sons, Moses finds himself with time to reflect on what he has seen and heard. So what is Moses's impression about God now? Certainly the scale is tipped to the side of God's severity.

Showdown on the Nile

Aaron came to meet Moses. The two of them boldly confronted Pharaoh and told him, "Thus says the Lord, the God of Israel,

'Let my people go.'" Pharaoh retorted: "Who is the LORD, that I should obey his voice and let Israel go? I do not know the LORD, and moreover, I will not let Israel go" (Ex. 5:1–2).

Pharaoh exercised his earthly sovereignty by demanding the same number of bricks without supplying the necessary materials for the already oppressed Israelites.

But God would have the last word: "Now you shall see what I will do to Pharaoh." God revealed His sovereignty by declaring four times, "I am the LORD" (Ex. 6:2, 6–8). He also shared seven wonderful "I will" statements in Exodus 3:7–21 to demonstrate his sovereignty over Pharaoh. God declared, "I will bring you out from under the burdens of the Egyptians, and I will deliver you from slavery to them, and I will redeem you with an outstretched arm and with great acts of judgment. I will take you to be my people, and I will be your God. . . . I will bring you into the land that I swore to Abraham, to Isaac, and to Jacob. I will give it to you for a possession." He also promised to bring them into the Promised Land and to give it to them.

Pharaoh's will was broken through a series of ten plagues demonstrating Yahweh's limitless power and sovereignty. Each plague was a direct assault on one of Egypt's gods, and each increased in intensity. The final plague took the life of every first-born Egyptian male—including Pharaoh's son. Pharaoh finally relented and released the Hebrews. His plaintive, last-minute request for a blessing, in Exodus 12:29–32, demonstrated how broken the once arrogant ruler had become. Israel carried the riches of Egypt with them as they made their exit—effectively receiving salary plus bonuses for their years of labor.

So after the showdown in Egypt, Moses and Israel were convinced that Yahweh was sovereign over everyone and everything. He was also personal and, best of all, He was on their side. Moses's relationship with God was growing stronger.

The Test

Authentic relationships are never static. They ebb and flow and hopefully grow deeper. After leaving Egypt, Israel experienced several more encounters with God. He displayed His presence and protective power in a cloud and a fiery pillar, demonstrating that He was there with them, 24/7.

Regardless of any warm feelings the Israelites might have had toward God after He had revealed Himself to them, it must have been quite a shock to them when He seemingly led them into a deadly trap by the Red Sea. The waters blocked their escape, and Egyptian war chariots were in hot pursuit. But God had already told Moses that this was His strategy, so that "the Egyptians shall know that I am the Lord" (Ex. 14:4).

Did Moses know that God planned to part the Red Sea as an escape route for His people? The Bible doesn't tell us. In that moment of great fear and panic, and possibly with as much confidence as he could muster, Moses tried to quiet the people by saying, "Fear not, stand firm, and see the salvation of the Lord, which he will work for you today. For the Egyptians whom you see today, you shall never see again. The Lord will fight for you, and you have only to be silent" (Ex. 14:13–14).

The angel of the Lord (the very One who had spoken to Moses from the burning bush) came between the Egyptians and Israel in the cloud. Waiting for daylight, the Egyptians had nothing to worry about, because the Israelites had no way to escape. Or so Pharaoh's army thought.

When Moses raised his staff, the sea parted, exposing terra firma. Illuminated by the fiery pillar, Israel crossed over during the night. Dawn revealed the pursuing Egyptians floundering in the sea while Israel sang in celebration and continued their journey. God provided fresh water to drink and set out a spread of "angel food" each morning.

Approximately three months after departing Egypt, the Israelites were camped near Mt. Sinai, a place that would earn the name "The Mountain of God." Up to this point, God had only spoken with Moses. Now it was Israel's turn to personally meet their God. But first He had a message for them in Exodus 19:4–6: "You yourselves have seen what I did to the Egyptians, and how I bore you on eagles' wings and brought you to myself. Now therefore, if you will indeed obey my voice and keep my covenant, you shall be my treasured possession among all peoples, for all the earth is mine; and you shall be to me a kingdom of priests and a holy nation."

God invited the people to hear His voice, but only after they had prepared and consecrated themselves. This audible encounter with the living God wasn't going to be a picnic in the park, and the Lord laid down some pretty strict ground rules. Could this be an expression of God's compassion on people who did not know the awesome glory of His person? Since God is far more glorious in power than the nuclear reaction we call our sun, His warnings are perfectly merciful. He will not diminish His glory because He is that He is.

Nobody but nobody was to even come close to touching the mountain where God would appear. Even the simplest infraction would result in immediate death.

Are you beginning to get the impression this was serious? Very serious indeed.

If I had been there, I would have been filled with dread and anticipation. The mountain was shrouded in smoke and "trembled greatly." And we thought the burning bush had been frightening!

God answered Moses with loud, rolling thunder. A

piercing, celestial trumpet blast grew relentlessly louder. Then God called Moses to meet with Him on the summit. Before his ascent, Moses once again warned the people to come no closer. So I ask, what is their impression of God now?

Moses remained on the mountain for an extended time receiving the Ten Commandments and other instructions. Moses's attention never wandered while God "laid down the law." But down at the bottom of the mountain, life returned to normal. With the people bored and already losing the adrenaline rush from the display on the mountain, things turned ugly.

Moses's attention never wandered while God "laid down the law." But down at the bottom of the mountain, life returned to normal.

While Moses was receiving laws forbidding making and worshiping idols, Aaron was skillfully forging a calf image. Worship of the bull, a familiar god back in Egypt, quickly evolved into an orgy. The culture of Egypt had shaped their view of God. Enflamed with an abundance of wine (which they must have spirited out of Egypt) and worshiping an impotent god of fertility, the party got way out of hand (Ex. 32). In fact, it would have made the Woodstock Festival look like a Sunday school picnic.

The strange, sad thing about the orgy below the mountain was that these people had just witnessed God's mighty miracles and had actually heard the thunder of His warnings. It ought to have been more than enough to put the fear of God in them. Soon enough, they would be reminded that God was holy when three thousand revelers perished by the sword and many others died from a raging plague. The tragic lesson that day was God will not be trivialized! God is severe. He is not safe.

Extended time in the presence of God had made Moses so

bold he would dare stand between the guilty nation and their very angry God. Moses said to the people, "You have sinned a great sin. And now I will go up to the LORD; perhaps I can make atonement for your sin" (Ex. 32:30).

Perhaps. It was certainly no sure thing, and Moses wanted this out-of-control multitude to understand that. Moses returned to meet with the Lord on Sinai. Listen to this amazing leader's unselfish and courageous conversation with God. "Alas, this people has sinned a great sin. They have constructed for themselves gods of gold. But now, if you will forgive their sin—but if not, please blot me out of your book that you have written" (Ex. 32:31–32).

This is not the same timid shepherd who shook like an autumn leaf in front of the burning bush! Moses now knows God well enough to stand "toe to toe" with Him.

Stop and consider what Moses is almost demanding God to do. This is not the same timid shepherd who shook like an autumn leaf in front of the burning bush! Moses now knows God well enough to stand "toe to toe" with Him.

God responded to Moses's almost irreverent demands. "Whoever has sinned against me, I will blot out of my book. But now go, lead the people to the place about which I have spoken to you; behold, my angel shall go before you. Nevertheless, in the day when I visit, I will visit their sin upon them" (Ex. 32:32–34).

Outside the camp, Moses had set up a tent where he, and often Joshua, would go to meet with God.

Whenever Moses entered the Tent of Meeting, the cloud moved in front of the door. "Thus the LORD used to speak with Moses face to face, as a man speaks to his friend" (Ex. 33:11). Moses became so comfortable, if that is the appropriate word, that he dared to pursue an even more intimate relationship with God. Listen to his request: "You have said, 'I know you by name, and you have also found favor in my sight.' Now therefore, if I have found favor in your sight, please show me now your ways, that I may know you" (vv. 12–13).

Not stopping with such a bold request, Moses dared to pressure God to not abandon the Israelites but to continue traveling with them. God agreed to do as Moses requested.

Having "won" a couple of concessions from God, Moses dared to push the envelope even further. I use the word *concession* to reflect Moses's perspective, but I realize God already knew in advance what Moses would ask. God didn't change His mind, but Moses was being changed through his dialogue with God.

We would expect God to start pushing back. "Moses, that's enough. Remember who you are talking to. We may be friends, but we're not buddies."

But listen to the Lord's response in Exodus 33:17: "This very thing that you have spoken I will do, for you have found favor in my sight, and I know you by name."

Moses, like a child begging his parent, persists even further: "Please show me your glory" (v. 18). There it is on the table in plain sight! "Let me see everything about You, God. No more secrets!"

God patiently responded, "I will make all my goodness pass before you and will proclaim before you my name 'The Lord.' And I will be gracious to whom I will be gracious, and will show mercy on whom I will show mercy. But *you cannot see my face, for man shall not see me and live*" (Ex. 33:19, emphasis mine).

Please take a moment to reflect on the preceding conversation between Moses and Yahweh. God will not be bullied or bribed by anyone, but He will go to shocking lengths to display His grace and mercy to whomever He chooses. And Moses was a chosen one. Perhaps the most profound declaration of God's holiness and glory is stated in this warning: *Nobody can look at God's face and live.* Just like we cannot look directly at the blazing sun without damaging our eyes, so we cannot see God in His totality and survive. We cannot survive without the sun, but the sun is not safe. Neither could we survive without the gracious gifts of God, but He is not safe!

God made a date with Moses. "Behold, there is a place by me where you shall stand on the rock, and while my glory passes by I will put you in a cleft of the rock, and I will cover you with my hand until I have passed by. Then I will take away my hand, and you shall see my back, but my face shall not be seen" (Ex. 33:21–23).

As the appointed day dawned, Moses no doubt arrived at the designated place on the mountain with his heart racing in anticipation. (Wouldn't yours?) For His part, God showed up right on schedule.

> The LORD descended in the cloud and stood with him there, and proclaimed the name of the LORD. The LORD passed before him and proclaimed, "The LORD, the LORD, a God merciful and gracious, slow to anger, and abounding in steadfast love and faithfulness, keeping steadfast love for thousands, forgiving iniquity and transgression and sin, but who will by no means clear the guilty, visiting the iniquity of the fathers on the children and the children's children, to the third and fourth generation." (Ex. 34:5–7)

Theologians call this passage God's self-disclosure. Note how God begins with His kinder, softer attributes. This is how

He wants to be remembered and worshiped. After igniting a bush to get Moses's attention and demanding he take off his sandals, after nearly killing Moses on the journey to Egypt, after frightening everybody with the thunder and piercing trumpet blast, and after eliminating more than three thousand out-of-control Israelites, God reveals Himself as compassionate, kind, patient, and forgiving!

We are not troubled over God's kinder attributes; in fact, we welcome them because we are all guilty and need grace and mercy.

God's self-disclosure is repeated eleven times in part or in total in the older testament.[2] God is patient and slow to anger; He is not malevolent or cruel. He is not quick to fly off the handle. He abounds in love and faithfulness. He never changes and is not capricious. He heaps love, loyal love, on thousands.

He is also holy and righteous and just. He will not leave the guilty unpunished. He is not a doting grandfather excusing bad behavior.

In this passage, both God's kindness and severity are on display. We are not troubled over God's kinder attributes; in fact, we welcome them because we are all guilty and need grace and mercy. We desire His patience, but God is also severe. Even so, lest we tip the scale too far toward His severity, look more closely at the text. Notice the contrast is between "God's love for thousands" and His justice on three or four generations. Notice also God's softer attributes are listed first, and the harsher warnings appear almost as an afterthought. Mercy and grace are always God's preference. You might call His love, compassion, and kindness God's default position.

That is another way of saying that God's very essence or nature is love. The apostle John said it this way in 1 John 4:8ff., "God is love." God not only loves us; He is love itself. He is the source of love. He is the perfect example of love that never gives up but gives unselfishly of Himself. God has demonstrated His love by sending "his Son to be the propitiation for our sins" (4:10). Christ dying in our place to satisfy the righteous demands of God is the greatest example of love. Is it not also a dramatic example of His holiness and His wrath against sin?

John Piper writes in *The Pleasures of God*, "His anger must be released by a stiff safety latch, but his mercy has a hair trigger."[3] You gun owners understand Piper's illustration. A gun has a safety built into it so that the trigger can't be pulled as long as the safety is on. A hair trigger is a gun that has a trigger that can be discharged at the slightest touch. It's dangerous. But in the case of God's love, the hair trigger is a welcome blessing and the stiff safety has spared us several times throughout our lives.

God's justice and mercy together have dealt with the offenses of our sin against His glorious holiness and have limited the devastating consequences that sin has caused on the human race.

Kindness and severity seem poles apart. Yet each word accurately describes God's nature. How can these two words describe the same person? That is the question addressed in the next chapter.

4

Kindness and Severity: Where They Meet

For the word of the Lord is upright,
and all his work is done in faithfulness.
He loves righteousness and justice;
the earth is full of the steadfast love of the Lord.

Psalm 33:4–5

Do you indeed decree what is right, you gods?
Do you judge the children of man uprightly? . . .
Mankind will say, "Surely there is a reward for the righteous;
Surely there is a God who judges on earth."

Psalm 58:1, 11

Prior to the total solar eclipse on August 21, 2017, central Oregon authorities were predicting a half-million excited viewers could make their way into our area. The "path of totality" (a term we became very familiar with) passed directly over Madras, a town forty-five miles north of my home in Bend.

Tourism helps drive our economy, with visitors drawn by the natural beauty, recreation opportunities, and abundant sunshine. As the day of the eclipse approached, local businesses anticipated increased sales from the influx of people. Predictably, some hotels raised their rates. Rooms in a motel in coastal Lincoln City that usually rented for $71 a night were listed at $999. Hospitals stocked up on medications and supplies. We were encouraged to fill our gas tanks in advance, because there would be very long lines or even a fuel shortage.

The Bend Bulletin, our local newspaper, ran an editorial titled "Tips to Survive the Eclipse." Along with all the precautions about the expected crowds of visitors, the most consistent and appropriate warning was "Do not look directly at the sun! Do not use ordinary sunglasses but only glasses approved to be safe."

I like lots of sunshine and welcome our beautiful sunsets over the Cascade Mountains. The sun warms us, cheers us, lights our way, and grows our crops. But the sun is also a mighty stellar engine of hydrogen and helium radiating vast amounts of energy. If you don't remember that, it might burn your skin or even blind you.

The sun isn't "safe," but the sun is wonderful. We can't live without it.

The same might be said about our God. In C. S. Lewis's *The Lion, the Witch and the Wardrobe*, we read this conversation between Mr. Beaver and Susan discussing a lion named Aslan, who represents Jesus Christ:

"... Aslan is a lion—*the* Lion, the great Lion."
"Ooh!" said Susan, "I'd thought he was a man. Is he—quite safe? I shall feel rather nervous about meeting a lion."
... "Safe? said Mr. Beaver; "... Who said anything about safe? 'Course he isn't safe. But he's good. He's the King, I tell you."[1]

Our God, the God who has revealed Himself in Scripture, has both gentle and harsh attributes. Perhaps these two contrasting character descriptions are never expressed more clearly than in Romans 11:22 where Paul writes about the *kindness and severity* of God. We might say, "Well then, I will relate to the kindness part." But we can't simply choose our favorite attribute of God and ignore the others. To do so is to insult His name and character.

In the older testament, a person's name (in this case God's name) revealed and included his character or nature. If God is both severe and kind, I must accept both attributes. He is to be loved, yes, but He is also to be feared and respected. So let's consider these two contrasting words: kindness and severity.

Severity

The best way to photograph a diamond is to present it on a black background. Under brilliant light, the vibrancy of the diamond is amazing.

Professionals use terms like brilliance, sparkle, and even fire to describe the radiance of this precious stone. I believe this is also true with God's softer attributes of grace, kindness, and mercy. We can't fully appreciate these more welcoming attributes without first considering God's more stern attributes.

Think about this for a moment. What adjective do we most often associate with God's grace? John Newton described it, "Amazing grace, how sweet the sound that saved a wretch like me."[2] The more Newton considered his own sinfulness in stark contrast to God's blazing holiness, the more he found grace to be simply amazing.

Charles Wesley used the same term. Contemplating the death of Christ in his place, he wrote, "Amazing love, how

59

can it be that Thou, my God, shouldst die for me!"³

"Amazing" has become a somewhat threadbare word these days. It's been used in our contemporary culture to describe so many things—from dish soap to breakfast cereal—that it no longer says much of anything. But what happens when you encounter something that truly soars above every attempt to wrap it in words? What term do you use? *Wondrous. Shocking. Startling. Stunning. Jaw-dropping.* When you begin to describe the holiness of God that demanded a death sentence on sinners, followed by the fact that Jesus, the Son of God Himself, died in our place to pay the penalty for us, it's hard to put that demonstration of love and grace into language.

Maybe the old word *amazing* serves as well as any.

When I hear someone say, "I love Jesus, but I don't like the angry God in the Old Testament," I cringe. Don't they know it is the same God in both testaments? The older testament introduces us to the God who rained down fire and brimstone on Sodom and also reveals the God who does justice and whose love is loyal and never changing.

> When I hear someone say, "I love Jesus, but I don't like the angry God in the Old Testament," I cringe. Don't they know it is the same God in both testaments?

I wonder if these critics of the older testament have considered the God who encouraged unfaithful Israel, "Can a woman forget her nursing child, that she should have no compassion on the son of her womb? Even these may forget, yet *I will not forget you. Behold, I have engraved you on the palms of my hands*" (Isa. 49:15–16, emphasis mine). What a graphic description of God's love and faithfulness.

God also invited Israel to "Come now, let us reason together, says the LORD: though your sins are like scarlet, they shall be as white as snow; though they are red like crimson, they shall become like wool" (Isa. 1:18). The same God, in Matthew 11:28, has invited anyone who is "weary and burdened" (NIV) to come to Him for rest. He has also sent invitations to you and me in John 7:37: "If anyone thirsts, let him come to me and drink."

Why am I considering God's severity before His kindness? Because this is the side of His nature and character that our contemporary culture most wants to paper over or ignore. It's easier and more pleasant to bask in His grace and kindness. But in so doing, we may forget that the grace God demonstrated when Jesus died on the cross came at a terrible price—demanded by white-hot holiness.

The word translated *severity* in Romans 11:22 in the ESV and the NASB is translated as *sternness* in the NIV. Sternness sounds a little less threatening than severity, doesn't it? (I would rather have a stern policeman stop me on the highway than a *severe* one!) *The Message* paraphrase makes the contrast between God's kindness and severity even more graphic: "Make sure you stay alert to these qualities of *gentle kindness* and *ruthless severity* that exist side by side in God—ruthless with the deadwood, gentle with the grafted shoot" (emphasis mine). "Deadwood" is a reference to the fruitless or sterile branches of an olive tree that have been cut off so that branches from a wild olive tree could be grafted into the stump of the old fruitless tree.

A note of caution is necessary in response to Eugene Peterson's use of the adjective *ruthless*. I believe Peterson chose the word to emphasize the extreme severity of God's response to Israel's disobedience, but technically the English word *ruthless* suggests cruelty or acting without mercy. That, of course, is not true of our God, who shows mercy even in His discipline. He is not cruel, but He is severe.

For example, in Romans 9–11 Paul addresses God's relationship with Israel after they had rejected their Messiah, Jesus. Had they crossed the line of no return, or would they get another "get out of jail free" card because they are Abraham's descendants? Were they exempt from God's judgment because they were still offering sacrifices at the temple?

The answer is a resounding *no*.

No amount of religious activities could atone for their grievous sin. They were cut off like a dead branch.

For a moment, let's consider the immediate context surrounding Romans 11:22. Romans 8 concludes with assurance that those who have been justified (pronounced righteous in Jesus Christ) cannot be severed from God's loyal love.

> No, in all these things we are more than conquerors through him who loved us. For I am sure that neither death nor life, nor angels nor rulers, nor things present nor things to come, nor powers, nor height nor depth, nor anything else in all creation, will be able to separate us from the love of God in Christ Jesus our Lord. (Rom. 8:37–39)

That certainly sounds secure, doesn't it? Nothing, absolutely nothing, can sever those who are in Christ Jesus from God's love. That's kindness.

But what about those who remain outside of Christ? That's where we encounter His severity. We discover in Romans 11 that unbelieving Israel who rejected Christ has been cut off or severed. The Jewish leaders not only rejected Jesus as their Messiah, but they persecuted anyone who dared to claim Jesus was the Christ.

Saul, once a persecutor of Christians, became one of the persecuted. Yet when he writes about God's harsh judgment upon Israel, he does so with off-the-charts concern for his people. He even states he would be willing to trade places with them: "I could wish that I myself were accursed and *cut off from Christ* for the sake of my brothers, my kinsmen according to the flesh" (Rom. 9:3). I have emphasized the words "cut off from" because they prepare us for the word *severity* in Romans 11:22.

I discovered that the word translated "severity" appears twice in verse 22—but never again in the entire Bible. That tweaked my curiosity. Why does Paul use this extremely rare word to describe God's wrath? Why doesn't he use one of the more common words such as wrath, anger, vengeance, or fury? To satisfy my curiosity I did a word study and came to the firm conclusion that Paul chose this rarely used word because it fits the context like no other word could have done.

Writing to Gentiles, Paul uses an olive tree to illustrate God's judgment on unbelieving Jews. The olive tree was one of the symbols for Israel in the older testament. Israel was God's chosen olive tree, and her fruit, her oil, was to be a blessing to the nations outside the covenant. However, in her pursuit to achieve righteousness through self-efforts and religious rituals, the olive tree had become barren, requiring severe measures from the master arborist.

Note the references to being cut off or broken in Romans 11:17–22:

But if some of the branches were broken off [literally, cut off], and you [Gentiles], although a wild olive shoot, were grafted in among the others and now share in the nourishing root of the olive tree, do not be arrogant toward the branches. If you are, remember it is not you who support the root, but the root that supports you. Then you will say, *"Branches were broken off* so that I might be grafted in." That is true. *They were broken off because of their unbelief,* but you stand fast through faith. So do not become proud, but fear. For if God did not spare the natural branches, neither will he spare you. *Note then the kindness and the severity of God: severity toward those who have fallen,* but God's kindness to you, provided you continue in his kindness. *Otherwise you too will be cut off.* (emphasis mine)

The noun translated *severity,* derived from a verb "to cut" or "to cut off" or "to circumcise," fits the illustration of cutting off worthless branches from an olive tree. I don't imagine the arborist being gentle with a dead or fruitless branch. If it was my olive tree, I would just get the worthless branch out of the way as quickly as possible! Perhaps, throw it in the back of the truck for a trip to the landfill.

I discovered Paul also uses an adjective that is related to our word *severity.* Writing with a very sharp pen in 2 Corinthians 13:2, Paul warns church leaders to deal with an internal problem, because "if I come again I will not spare them." Paul seems to raise the temperature in verse 10: "For this reason I write these things while I am away from you, that when I come I may not have to *be severe* [to act severely or harshly] in my use of the authority that the Lord has given me."

Paul also warned Titus to confront false teachers: "For there are many who are insubordinate, empty talkers and deceivers, especially those of the circumcision party. They must be silenced. . . . Therefore *rebuke them sharply,* that they may be sound in the faith" (Titus 1:10–11a, 13, emphasis mine).

Severity fits the context of cutting off faithless Israel. In contrast, we also see God's kindness when He grafts wild branches or Gentiles into the privileged place once occupied by Israelites. Once again, I point out how Eugene Peterson's *The*

Message makes the contrast vivid: *"gentle kindness and ruthless severity."*

We cannot ignore either God's severity or His kindness; both are necessary. You and I wouldn't want (as if we had a choice) a syrupy-sweet God who never expresses anger or never metes out judgment on anybody. We don't want a God who passively sits by watching horrible acts of injustice being carried out on the weak and vulnerable but never lifts a finger or raises His voice to administer justice. The psalms of lament are the most common genre of psalms for a reason. When the wicked seem to go scot-free, we want God to administer justice.

You and I wouldn't want (as if we had a choice) a syrupy-sweet God who never expresses anger or never metes out judgment on anybody.

Anger is the natural response to injustice, and such anger isn't sinful. We might even call it "righteous anger." It has been said, and is true, that the opposite of anger is not love but apathy. To see horrible injustice being done to an innocent child and not express anger is not only wrong; it is evil.

That is the reason behind the imprecatory psalms in the Bible. The composers of these psalms have experienced or witnessed terrible injustice, and they want God to avenge them. Just this morning as I was reading the Psalms, I discovered another imprecatory psalm expressing severe anger and a desire for revenge. David, in Psalm 58, calls on God to punish the wicked persons. He concludes the psalm with, "Mankind will say, 'Surely there is reward for the righteous; surely there is a God who judges on earth.'" I agree with David and wouldn't want it any other way.

As I write, the parents of a five-year-old adopted daughter are facing trial. When I first learned that little Maria (not her real name) had died from emaciation resulting from her parents allegedly withholding food and medical attention from their little girl, I recoiled with anger. Because my mind has been made up, I suspect I could never qualify to sit on the jury for this case. *Throw the book at them!* I demand justice for Maria.

In a nearby town another couple has been charged with physically abusing their two-year-old daughter, who has apparently suffered several fractures and other injuries. It has also been alleged that she had been left alone in her home with heroin and methamphetamine present. If I don't feel anger at the injustice done to these innocent children, if I just shrug my shoulders and turn to the comic page, I am to be pitied. By the same token, if God doesn't feel compassion for this little victim of abuse, or if He doesn't express anger, *He isn't good nor would He be God.*

I want a God who cares enough and loves deeply enough to punish those who commit such injustice.

I have visited Yad Vashem, the Holocaust memorial in Jerusalem, several times. Recently my wife and I visited the Holocaust Museum in Washington, D.C., where I was reminded of the indescribable crimes against humanity that had been done under the banner of the swastika, which has become a symbol of hatred and bigotry.

Walking through the museum left an indelible imprint on my mind—perhaps the most significant being that *somebody must answer* for these atrocities. Maybe I am revealing my more vengeful side, but I am grateful to know there will be a judgment day when even those who avoided facing human war-crime tribunals—whether through suicide or escaping to South America—will be held accountable. At the highest tribunal of all.

It is safe to say that no reform movement has ever begun

or succeeded unless it was motivated by anger over injustice. Righteous anger drove the abolition movement against the evils of slavery. Anger also led the efforts to eliminate abuses of child labor during the Industrial Revolution. It was justified anger that drove the Civil Rights movement to resist the injustice of segregation in America and apartheid in South Africa. Today, godly anger is driving the fight against human trafficking.

If it was not for anger, this world would be run by tyrants even more than it has been. Apart from righteous anger, nobody would be safe anywhere in this world. Ever!

It is safe to say that no reform movement has ever begun or succeeded unless it was motivated by anger over injustice.

I discovered another possible reason that Paul used this rare word translated *severity*. A secular manuscript from the first century speaks of an attorney who was defending a very harsh legal sentence. He claims the law was enforced "rigidly"—the same word translated "severity" in Romans. In other words, the punishment had been as severe as it could possibly be under the Law.[4] I believe Paul chose this rare word not only because it fits the context of cutting off Israel from her privileged place, but also because it suggests the sentence upon Israel was carried out to the fullest extent of the Law.

When Jesus triumphantly rode a donkey into Jerusalem, He was greeted by an exuberant multitude waving branches and shouting praises fit for the Messiah. According to Luke 19:39–40, some Pharisees asked Him to "rebuke" His disciples. They wanted Him to put an end to the messianic nonsense. Jesus responded, "I tell you [or listen up!], if these [people in the crowd] were silent, the very stones would cry out."

To understand the above statement about stones crying

out, we must read the next paragraph in Luke. As Jesus approached the city, He wept over it and prophesied that Jerusalem would someday be laid under siege and devastated along with its citizens. The reason? Jesus said it was "because you did not know the time of your visitation." In other words, rejecting Jesus as the legitimate Messiah sealed the destruction of the city and the religious system as they knew it.

God had once sentenced unfaithful Judah to seventy years captivity in Babylon for her love affair with idolatry. Being carried into exile was exactly what Moses warned God would do if Israel ever turned away from Him to worship idols (Deut. 4:15–31). Deuteronomy 28 is an extensive list of blessings and curses Israel could expect depending on whether they obeyed God or not.

The chapter closes with the harshest sentence of all; Israel would be forcefully dispersed among the nations, where they would languish in servitude. Heaven and earth were called in as witnesses to the covenant God made with Israel. "I have set before you life and death, blessing and curse. Therefore choose life, that you and your offspring may live, loving the Lord your God, obeying his voice and holding fast to him, for he is your life and length of days, that you may dwell in the land" (Deut. 30:19–20).

Now, if God punished Judah to the fullest extent of the Law for the sin of idolatry, what sentence would be appropriate for rejecting God's Son? The Jewish religious leaders exchanged Jesus for a common criminal, Barabbas. They handed Jesus over to the pagan Roman authorities, insisting He be crucified even though Pilate tried to appeal to their sense of honor and justice.

For this sin, Israel was not exiled for seven decades but was severely cut off, uprooted from the land God had given them, and dispersed among the nations.

To this day the temple lies in ruins, replaced by an Islamic mosque . . . and we begin to understand the import of Paul's words, when he said, "Behold the severity of God."

There is another, more positive, reason the temple lies in ruins today. It is no longer necessary, because Jesus has become the perfect and permanent High Priest who offered Himself as the perfect sacrifice for all sins once for all. Bloody sacrifices are no longer needed. They have been discarded like a rotten orange.

Remember when I spoke about a priceless, multifaceted diamond resting against a black background? What I have just detailed is that black background.

And now . . . it's time to look at the diamond.

Kindness

Our God is not like Jekyll and Hyde. He doesn't have good days and bad days (or good millennia and bad millennia). In fact, His two seemingly incompatible attributes, severity and kindness, are perfectly blended in one absolutely profound person who is worthy of our praise.

God's loyal love and His awesome wrath are frequently juxtaposed throughout Scripture, such as in John 3:16, 36 and Romans 5:8. Paul, for another example, after using six words to describe the wrong use of anger in Ephesians 4:31, immediately challenges us to be "kind to one another,

> **Our God is not a schizophrenic Jekyll and Hyde. He doesn't have good days and bad days (or good millennia and bad millennia).**

tenderhearted, forgiving one another, as God in Christ forgave you" (v. 32).

The word translated *kind* in Ephesians 4:32 is the same word translated *kindness* in Romans 11:22. Kindness is rooted in the word *grace*. Although kindness is not a verb, it is an action word. It's not just something you are, it is something you do. Ephesians 2:7 tells us that God's immeasurable grace was demonstrated in "kindness toward us." Because Jesus was kind by nature, "He went about doing good and healing all" (Acts 10:38). Jesus also said, "A good person produces good things from the treasury of a good heart" (Luke 6:45 NLT). In other words, you can't be "good" by doing nothing.

That would make you good for nothing!

Randy, a pastor friend of mine, was my prayer partner for almost twenty years before he moved to Portland. The motto of New Hope Church, where Randy pastored, was "Grace in Action." That's a great definition for the word *kindness*.

Kindness is to be good, pleasant, and gracious. It is the extreme contrast to harshness and severity.

The last memorial service I led at Foundry Church was for one of our deaconesses, Edell. When we gave those in attendance the opportunity to share memories, we heard over and over that she was "the kindest and sweetest person" they had ever met. To this day, I can close my eyes and see her smile. I cherish the memory of her disposition. While battling pancreatic cancer in its latter stage, Edell's gentle spirit continued to shine through the pain.

Just a few weeks before her death, she attended a worship service, and I greeted her in the foyer. Although very weak, she smiled and we hugged. That would be our final hug, but the fragrance of her faith and the sweetness of her character lingers. With that in mind, I chose 2 Corinthians 2:14–16 as the text for her memorial service.

Take a moment to savor these words from *The Living Bible*:

But thanks be to God! For through what Christ has done, he has triumphed over us so that now wherever we go he uses us to tell others about the Lord and to spread the Gospel like a sweet perfume. As far as God is concerned there is a sweet, wholesome fragrance in our lives. It is the fragrance of Christ within us. (2 Cor. 2:14–15)

The fragrance of Christ! What better thing could be said about anyone, anywhere? But as precious as the fragrance of Edell's love for Jesus was, nothing can compare to the fragrance of God's kindness demonstrated to us in Christ.

I share one more example of our word *kindness* from Titus 3:4, where two similar words are stacked upon each other for emphasis. Paul writes: "But when the goodness and loving kindness of God our Savior appeared, he saved us."

The word translated *goodness* here is the same word translated *kindness* in Romans 11:22.

The second word in Titus 3:4, translated "loving kindness," is the Greek word *philanthropia*, derived from two words: "love people." Sounds like our English word *philanthropy*, doesn't it? Paul uses the word to describe God's unselfish love for mankind.

The same word appears in Acts 27:3, where it has the connotation of showing courtesy to another person—especially someone considered to be inferior. Julius, the Roman centurion charged with delivering Paul to stand trial in Rome, "treated Paul kindly." Luke uses the same word, *philanthropia*, in Acts 28:2 to describe how "The native people showed us *unusual kindness*, for they kindled a fire and welcomed us all." After Paul and his fellow travelers were shipwrecked, the islanders welcomed the survivors and treated them as family, not as strangers.

To be philanthropic in our culture is to be generous or to respond to needs by sharing resources without any expectation of personal gain. Many wonderful deeds such as famine relief, providing clean, potable water, and basic medical care are being done around the world today by affluent philanthropists.

But none of these, for all their millions or billions invested in worthy ways, can compare with our God, the greatest philanthropist of all. He didn't just give out of His abundance, *He gave Himself.* Has it ever been stated more eloquently than John 3:16? "God so loved the world, that he gave his only Son, that whoever believes in him should not perish but have eternal life."

Paul added his description of this love in Romans 5:7–8: "For one will scarcely die for a righteous person—though perhaps for a good person one would dare even to die—but God shows his love for us in that while we were still sinners, Christ died for us."

You and I are the recipients of the greatest philanthropic love gift ever!

In August 2017, Hurricane Harvey devastated the city of Houston, southeastern Texas, and western Louisiana. Torrential rain—almost a year's worth—fell in just a few days, wreaking havoc, taking lives, displacing thousands, and destroying billions of dollars of property. By any standard this was a severe weather phenomenon. Some would even call it an "act of God," but that is not to say God was pouring out wrath on Houston.

I don't know why Hurricane Harvey made landfall where it did or why it just hung up there, recycling storm after devastating rainstorm. But we all agree it was a severe disaster. Hurricane Irma soon followed, blasting apart homes, businesses, and lives in the Caribbean, Florida, and several states. Irma was followed by yet additional hurricanes in the Caribbean.

Thankfully, after these natural disasters, we witnessed an outpouring of love and generous philanthropic deeds.

Black people rescued white people and vice versa. Conservatives and progressives locked arms to assist victims. Democrats and Republicans reached across the aisle to fund FEMA. We witnessed both severity and kindness in an amazing balance. Perhaps both the storms *and* the following rivers of help, compassion, and kindness were "acts of God."

The truth is, we human beings with our finite minds can never begin to explain a God like the God of the Bible. How can we place His stunning severity alongside His unspeakable kindness and grace and try to build a bridge between the two?

We can't. We falter and fail every time we try.

But then again, we don't need to. God Himself has given us that bridge, that perfect balance of all He is.

His name is Jesus. We will meet Him up close and personal in the next chapter. We will consider both the tender healing touch of His hand and His strong arm bearing a sword as He metes out severe judgment.

5

Lion and Lamb

*And they were bringing children to him that he might touch
them, and the disciples rebuked them. But when Jesus saw it,
he was indignant and said to them, "Let the children come
to me; do not hinder them, for to such belongs the kingdom of
God. Truly, I say to you, whoever does not receive the kingdom
of God like a child shall not enter it." And he took them in his
arms and blessed them, laying his hands on them.*

Mark 10:13–16

*And no one in heaven or on earth or under the earth was able
to open the scroll or to look into it, and I began to weep loudly.
. . . And one of the elders said to me, "Weep no more; behold, the
Lion of the tribe of Judah, the Root of David, has conquered, so
that he can open the scroll and its seven seals." And between the
throne and the four living creatures and among the elders I saw
a Lamb standing, as though it had been slain.*

Revelation 5:3–6a

"What's your favorite picture of Jesus?"

I tossed out the question to the men at The Shepherd's
House, a faith-based recovery ministry, as we began a study of
the gospel of Luke.

Growing up, it seemed to me that every home I entered had a picture of Warner Sallman's *Head of Christ*. If you grew up attending Sunday school or had devout parents or grandparents, you've no doubt seen it yourself. Sallman created a somewhat effeminate image of Jesus, with long, wavy brown hair and a sharply pointed nose. In the picture, He seems to have unfocused eyes, gazing vacantly off at some point beyond the viewer's right shoulder.

Sallman was a commercial artist in Chicago who found fame depicting Jesus in a series of paintings. The *Head of Christ* painting sold more than 500 million copies. Perhaps a close second to Sallman's portrait of Jesus was Bernhard Plockhorst's *Good Shepherd*. Plockhorst, a nineteenth-century German artist, portrays Jesus with long, soft, brown hair, clearly European features, clothed in a beautiful maroon robe. He carries a lamb in His right arm and a shepherd's staff in His left. The snow-white lamb looks as though its little hooves have never touched earth, while a flock of adult sheep are staring blissfully up at the shepherd as he walks barefoot through the countryside.

The picture never connected with me, a farm boy. Our sheep never looked up at us with admiration. And no one would have walked barefoot through the pastures of my youth—unless they enjoyed treading on sand burrs.

Recently I discovered a painting on the internet titled, *Rejoice*. Randy Friemel, the artist, painted a masculine Jesus with a weathered face and a broad smile—just about to break into laughter—with a lamb wrapped around His shoulders. Now, I like that picture!

One of the first songs many of us learned as a child was "Jesus loves me, this I know." This was the Jesus many of us learned to love. But was Jesus always meek and mild, or did

He have a stern streak? I invite you to pull out the album as we compare two dramatically different pictures of Him—a gentle lamb and a fierce lion.

Which Jesus?

We all love the kinder, gentler Jesus, friend to little children, destitute widows, and the desperately ill. Churches used to sing a chorus with these words: "Jesus is the sweetest name I know, and He's just the same as His lovely name."[1]

In the book of Revelation, however, we meet someone far, far beyond sweet and lovely. In fact, He is the most severe, intense, overwhelming person we could begin to imagine. As our planet's history winds to a close, we are given a terrifying picture in Revelation 6:15–16:

> Then the kings of the earth and the great ones and the generals and the rich and the powerful, and everyone, slave and free, hid themselves in the caves and among the rocks of the mountains, calling to the mountains and rocks, "Fall on us and hide us from the face of him who is seated on the throne, and from the wrath of the Lamb."

Which Jesus is real? Which portrayal is accurate?

In fact, both of them.

So I invite you to join me on a journey through biblical history to discover these two attributes of God: kindness and severity juxtaposed side by side in perfect balance in the person of Jesus Christ.

Our first photo stop is Genesis 2–3. Everything was good in paradise until Adam and Eve rejected God's goodness by listening to the serpent's slanderous lie that they would become like God if they would simply disobey. God's severe response resulted in the invasion of suffering, pain, and death as well as banishment. God drove them out of the garden and placed the powerful cherubim and a flaming sword to prevent their return.

Banishment. Exile. A "flaming sword that turned every way to guard the way to the tree of life" (Gen. 3:24). That sounds severe to me, but God also responded with mercy by preventing Adam and Eve from eating of the Tree of Life and sealing their doom to be forever alienated from their Creator!

God could have destroyed the rebels on the spot. It was His right as Creator, and it would have been a righteous response.

But it could have been worse. God could have destroyed the rebels on the spot. It was His right as Creator, and it would have been a righteous response. But in kindness, God sought out the rebels and provided animal skins for a covering.

G. Campbell Morgan once explained that the reason we fear God is not due to His nature, but it is in ourselves. Throughout the Bible, people like Moses who knew God most intimately had the least fear of Him, yet never lost their deep respect of God. As Proverbs tells us, "the fear of the LORD is the beginning of wisdom" (9:10). But it isn't a cringing fear, like a child might have toward an abusive father, but a reverent awe as toward a strong but loving and dependable daddy.

Morgan observed that God's first question recorded in Scripture, "Where are you?" was very revealing: "It was not the call of a policeman arresting a criminal. It is rather the wail of a father, who had lost his child."[2]

Adam hid because of his sin and shame. He was also genuinely afraid—as he should have been! But just a few verses later, God's kindness and grace blazed forth, displayed in His promise that the seed of the woman would someday destroy the works of the serpent.

We know that seed—the promised Redeemer—to be Jesus Christ.

The next photo of God's kindness and severity is the universal flood in Genesis 9–11. I don't need to point out God's severity in the flood. But you may ask, "Where is the *kindness*, when every person on earth except Noah's family perished?" We must remember, however, the flood was not a surprise attack on innocent and uninformed people. God had provided both an oral warning of the impending judgment through Noah's persistent preaching and a visual warning through the construction of the ark for 120 years. God offered a window of *120 years* for anyone who would repent and be spared.

In 2017, our nation and the surrounding countries endured a very severe hurricane season, but nobody should have been caught by surprise. We knew about the storms and had given them names while they were still out in the Atlantic several weeks away from landfall. In some cases, officials went door to door, warning and pleading with residents to evacuate.

Some did, fleeing to higher ground. Some did not, and some of those perished.

In Noah's day, without divine intervention, wickedness would have infected the entire human race and there would be no promised Seed. No Redeemer. No salvation. No hope. By sparing righteous Noah, God preserved that seed. Jesus Christ is a descendant of Noah, as demonstrated in Jesus' genealogy in Luke 3:36.

The destruction of Sodom was also a dramatic display of God's severity. But the fact God accepted Abraham's request to spare Sodom for just ten righteous citizens is evidence of God's patience and mercy. Another example of God's severity and kindness was the Exodus. Israel was released from bondage by the strong hand of God. He led them, fed them, and protected them throughout their journey, even though time after time they questioned Him, complained against Him, and out-and-out disobeyed Him. Eventually, they entered the Promised Land. Before they got there, God displayed His severity when an entire generation perished in the wilderness, and the trip that should have taken a few months became forty miserable, tedious, and dusty years.

I think I can hear somebody pushing back a little at this point, saying that those pictures of a severe God are strictly *Old Testament* images. Yes they are, but let me respond. We do not meet two gods in the Bible, nor is Jesus just a more gentle face on the God of the older testament. Jesus was fully God in every way.

We worship the triune God. Everything God has ever done, whether creating the universe or punishing Sodom, was done in unison by the Father, the Son, and the Holy Spirit. Jesus never acted apart from the Father.

Back to the Photo Album

So again, what image of Jesus in the Gospels do you identify with the most? What is your favorite biblical picture of Jesus? Is it the shepherd carrying the lamb close to His chest? Or is it the one where Jesus holds a little girl in His lap, tousling her hair?

Perhaps you have seen the Christmas card with the picture of a newborn infant's tiny hand reaching out from a manger. In that tiny hand, I see a helpless baby. Yes, but I also see the strong arm of the Creator reaching out to rescue me.

I can see Jesus kneeling to write in the dirt while the immoral woman's accusers slip away with shame burning on their faces. (See John 7:53–8:11.) Oh, to have also seen Jesus reaching out with compassion to touch a man in the late stages of leprosy—a man who has not felt the warm comfort of human touch for years—while the crowd gasps!

Wow, how many pictures we could paint of Jesus meek and mild, full of tenderness and compassion! The four gospels are saturated with such snapshots. Multitudes flocked to witness this man of Galilee who loved little children and sinners. One government official, Zacchaeus, scrambled up into a tree just to see Jesus pass by. When Jesus saw Zacchaeus in the tree, He invited Himself to share a meal at the tax collector's home. You can read the story in Luke 19:1–10.

But Jesus didn't always act like a meek lamb. He is also portrayed as a lion.

Not an old gray-bearded, declawed, and toothless lion lounging in a zoo, but a roaring wild lion, the king of the beasts with fangs exposed and ears bent backward and tail twitching while He prepares to devour an enemy that has dared to invade His territory. That fierce lion is also my Jesus and yours.

On our last ministry trip to Uganda, we were fortunate to watch two male lions resting in the tall grass in Queen Elizabeth National Park. They seemed to pose for us as we took several pictures of these majestic beasts. To make the setting even more surreal, a herd of buffalo grazed tranquilly in the distance. Soon the entire herd began to charge the lions. I could almost sense the ground rumbling under the hooves of these impressive beasts as the lions literally hightailed across the savanna into a nearby forest.

That's not the Lion of the tribe of Judah.

He fears nothing.

He flees from nobody.

He is not King in name only. It isn't a courtesy title. He *is* the King above all earthly kings. Jesus is the one true King who treads through the pages of Scripture.

Mark describes Jesus' indignation after His disciples rebuked parents for bringing their children to Him. Jesus publicly shamed His disciples and took the babies in his arms and blessed them (Luke 18:15–17). Imagine it, He stopped to cuddle little children with runny noses and dirty diapers. That's my Jesus.

I see the lion snarling as He called the religious leaders hypocrites, snakes, and stinking graves. In Matthew 23, Jesus pronounced seven woes or threats on the religious leaders. I see the lion in Jesus as He comes with a whip, face raging with anger as He upsets the money changers' tables in the temple, releasing the sacrificial animals while driving out the men who dared to pollute His Father's house. He treated them like the thieves they were. That's not Jesus meek and mild; this was the lion reclaiming his rightful lair. That's my Jesus.

The Lion in Revelation

But if you really want to meet Jesus the lion up close and personal, stroll through the last book in the Bible. I realize there have been several approaches to interpreting Revelation. But, regardless of how you interpret the book, you come face-to-face

Regardless of how you interpret Revelation, you come face to face with Jesus.

with Jesus. Note the first words in chapter 1: "The revelation of Jesus Christ." Here is a full unveiling of Jesus Christ in all His glory and majesty, Lamb of God and Lion of Judah.

Revelation 1:4–5 is a doxology to our triune God. The Father is eternal. The Holy Spirit is described as perfect in the phrase "the seven spirits." The number seven is frequently used in Scripture to describe perfection. Verse 5 offers three descriptive statements about Jesus: the faithful witness or martyr, the firstborn from the dead, and the ruler over all earthly kings.

A martyr tells the truth even if it means death. Stephen is called a martyr in Acts 22:20. Jesus called Antipas "my faithful witness, who was killed among you" (Rev. 2:13). Revelation 17:6 refers to the "blood of the saints, the blood of the martyrs of Jesus." Jesus is the faithful witness because He too was a martyr. Here was a person who could have avoided death without recanting His claims to be God because He had the power at His disposal to destroy His enemies and accusers.

But He didn't. Thank God a million times over that He didn't!

Jesus is called the "firstborn of the dead" because He conquered death and demonstrated absolute power over it.

Jesus is called "the ruler of kings on earth" because He is greater than and has sovereignty over all earthly leaders— whether kings, queens, dictators, presidents, or prime ministers. The image of Jesus as the King of kings in Revelation 19:11–16 is frighteningly severe.

Got your camera ready? Consider Jesus as He walks among the seven churches in Revelation 1:12–16. He is clothed with a long robe with a golden sash around His chest. We use the word *like* when we try to describe something that is indescribable. Jesus is described as having hair white *like* snow and eyes *like* flaming fire and feet "*like* burnished bronze, refined in a furnace, and his voice was *like* the roar of many waters. In his right hand he held seven stars, from his mouth came a sharp two-edged sword, and his face was *like* the sun shining in full strength" (emphasis mine).

This certainly doesn't look like the soft-robed, barefoot Jesus in the painting, strolling among the admiring sheep. And this also doesn't resemble the meek Jesus who stood silently while soldiers mocked Him and crushed a crown of tearing thorns onto His skull.

This is the regal lion.

If I had been there, like John, I would have also fallen at His feet as a dead man. There would have been two of us lying there insensible. His face, John said, was "like the sun shining in full strength." From our backyard in Bend we saw 99.7 percent of the sun blocked during the eclipse in 2017. The sun had virtually disappeared, but I still couldn't look directly at it without protective glasses—even though only .3 percent of the sun was revealed. John describes Jesus' face as brilliant as the midsummer sun at high noon. That is bright—a white, searing radiance intense enough to blind—and that is my Jesus.

The Jesus we love to love was criticized for being a friend of sinners, and He proudly wore the title with equal dignity. But the Lion of Judah walking among His churches in Revelation is both severe and kind. Pause and read Revelation 2 and 3 to discover Jesus' words of encouragement and/or of warning to each of the seven churches.

He commends each church for any good that remains within them and also warns of severe judgment if they refuse to repent and return wholeheartedly. He threatens to totally remove the lampstand of the church at Ephesus. He warned Pergamum to repent or "I will come soon and war against them with the sword of my mouth."

If these words don't sound severe, then consider this warning to Thyatira: "I will throw her onto a sickbed. . . . I will strike her children dead." And to Sardis, you'd better repent, Jesus said, or "I will come like a thief . . . I will come against you." Finally, to Laodicea, "Because you are lukewarm, and neither hot nor cold, I will spit you out of my mouth. . . . Repent. Behold,

I stand at the door and knock. If anyone hears my voice and opens the door [repents and returns], I will come in to him and eat with him, and he with me."

The tragedy of that threat—and it's not an invitation to sit down over a cup of joe at Starbucks—is that Jesus is *outside* the church knocking and knocking . . . and they don't even miss Him! The precious part is that Jesus still welcomed any member of the church of Laodicea who chose to repent and return to Him.

How clearly these truths are presented in the first three chapters of Revelation. It's so easy to identify both Jesus' kindness and severity displayed in His letters to these seven first-century churches.

He's the Lion and the Lamb.

He is not safe, but He is good.

> **The tragedy of that threat—and it's not an invitation to sit down over a cup of joe at Starbucks—is that Jesus is *outside* the church knocking and knocking . . . and they don't even miss Him!**

The Lamb in Revelation

The scene changes in Revelation 4, where we are invited into the very throne room in heaven. I love how John writes, "I looked, and there before me was a door standing open in heaven" (Rev. 4:1 NIV). That says to me that heaven is not impossibly distant from us in a galaxy far, far away. It is near! Perhaps all around us, just beyond sight.

The worship we experience in Revelation 4 ought to stir our hearts. And once more, John can't begin to wrap words around what he witnesses in that moment. Once again he has to use the word *like* to try to describe something and Someone too glorious for human speech. Our attention is drawn to the

One sitting on the throne. Surrounding the great throne are angels and redeemed humans saying, "Holy, holy, holy is the Lord God Almighty, who was and is and is to come!" (v. 8). Everyone falls before Him in wonder, and sings, "Worthy are you, our Lord and God, to receive glory and honor and power, for you created all things, and by your will they existed and were created" (v. 11).

The focus in chapter 5 is upon the person sitting to the right of God the Father. John begins to weep because nobody in heaven or on earth or even under the earth is qualified to open the seals of the great scroll. Then John hears these comforting words, "Weep no more; behold, the Lion of the tribe of Judah, the Root of David, has conquered, so that he can open the scroll and its seven seals" (v. 5).

There in the throne room John saw "a Lamb standing, as though it had been slain" (Rev. 5:6). Angels and the redeemed fall before the Lamb singing, "Worthy are you to take the scroll and to open its seals, for you were slain, and by your blood you ransomed people for God from every tribe and language and people and nation, and you have made them a kingdom and priests to our God, and they shall reign on the earth" (vv. 9–10).

If that scene hasn't sent chills down our spines, John also reports that "myriads of myriads and thousands of thousands" (v. 11) sang loudly, "Worthy is the Lamb who was slain, to receive power and wealth and wisdom and might and honor and glory and blessing!" (v. 12). John heard additional voices joining the choir as "every creature in heaven and on earth and under the earth and in the sea, all that is in them, saying 'To him who sits on the throne and to the Lamb be blessing and honor and glory and might forever and ever!'" (v. 13).

The praise in chapters 4 and 5 is in response to God's creative power and mercy. However, the focus soon turns from

Jesus' love and compassion to His wrath as the seals on the scroll are peeled back to reveal severe judgments.

After the fifth seal was broken, John saw "the souls of those who had been slain for the word of God and for the witness they had borne" (Rev. 6:9) crying out "how long before you will judge and avenge our blood on those who dwell on the earth?" (v. 10). This brief prayer of lament, "How long?" sets the stage for the rest of the book as the Lamb, now a roaring Lion, avenges innocent blood.

Chapter 7, however, also reveals God's kindness as we are introduced to a seemingly endless throng, from every nation and tribal group, who are clothed in white robes as they worship the Lamb who has avenged their innocent blood. John reports in Revelation 7:15–17 that they "have washed their robes and made them white in the blood of the Lamb."

They are before the throne of God, and serve him day and night in his temple; and he who sits on the throne will shelter them with his presence. They shall hunger no more, neither thirst anymore; the sun shall not strike them, nor any scorching heat. For the Lamb in the midst of the throne will be their shepherd, and he will guide them to springs of living water, and God will wipe away every tear from their eyes.

As I read those verses, I hear echoes from David's familiar psalm declaring the Lord is his shepherd, so he lacks nothing.

The severe judgments continue to intensify like the plagues God unleashed upon Egypt in the book of Exodus. Then another spontaneous burst of praise is recorded in Revelation 11:15: "The kingdom of the world has become the kingdom of our Lord and of his Christ, and he shall reign forever and ever."

Those words usher me back to my days at the Moody Bible Institute when I first heard and sang Handel's *Messiah*. Now, at this stage in my life, those same words pull me into the future, for I also am asking, "O Lord, how long? How much longer before You return to unleash righteous anger and avenge the blood of the innocent?"

The last judgment recorded in Revelation 16–18 may be the most severe in all Scripture, as God makes Babylon "drain the cup of the wine of the fury of his wrath" (Rev. 16:19). Babylon is a symbol for all human efforts to build a kingdom on earth without God. It is secular humanism at its very core. Today we are experiencing Babylon's hatred of God and biblical morality.

Remember Peter Hitchens, the British journalist and one-time atheist I mentioned earlier? He offers an explanation for the hostility toward Christianity:

> Christian belief, by subjecting all men to divine authority and by asserting in the words, "My kingdom is not of this world," that the ideal society does not exist in this life, is the most coherent and potent obstacle to secular utopianism.... The concepts of sin, of conscience, of eternal life, and of divine justice under unalterable law are the ultimate defense against the utopians' belief that the ends justify the means and that morality is relative.[4]

We recognized the spirit of Babylon in Soviet and Maoist Communism's efforts to exterminate the church and Christianity. But do we recognize Babylon's selfish thirst for power and wealth in our own culture's materialism, even when it comes at the expense of exploiting the weak and vulnerable? There are only two competing kingdoms in human history—the kingdom of God and the kingdom of Babylon.

Followers of Jesus are encouraged by His promise: "I will build my church, and the gates of hell shall not prevail against it" (Matt. 16:18).

There are only two competing kingdoms in human history— the kingdom of God and the kingdom of Babylon.

The early church, though small and seemingly insignificant and without rights, survived Rome's oppression and exploded across all geographical and political borders. Paul wrote, "The gospel is bearing fruit and growing throughout the whole world—just as it has been doing" (Col. 1:6 NIV).

Today, the powerful earthly kingdom of Babylon buzzes with the sounds of industry and commerce. Babylon seems indestructible. She rants against God while declaring her independence, but God will have the last word. In the description of Babylon's dramatic fall in Revelation 16:21, the people curse God right down to the bitter end, even while experiencing His judgment. Read the funeral dirge over Babylon's fall in Revelation 18. Her splendor has become rubble. No more music is to be heard in her streets. Her factories lie silent. (This will be the greatest "Rust Belt" in history.) And finally, best of all, there will be no more martyrs' blood spilled in her, according to Revelation 21:1–4.

I offer a contemporary example of God's patience and kindness. America enjoys God's bounty in spite of our sinfulness. If God responded in His severe wrath as we deserve, I would certainly fear for America's survival. God cares about the weak and vulnerable and promises to avenge innocent blood, yet we have sacrificed 60 million innocents to the god of personal freedom and pleasure. The very word *marriage* has been defiled. What God condemns has been made the law of the land. What God calls evil is now considered normal and good. When the White House was lit with the colors of the rainbow to celebrate the law that redefines marriage, did America cross the line? When will God's severity fall on us?

Certainly God has just cause. He consistently required Israel to care for the widow, the poor, and all who were most vulnerable. We are instructed to do the same as followers of Jesus. If Israel had followed the laws of the covenant, there would have been less reason for poverty among them. Even the law of gleaning was a built-in protection for the poor.

Have we, today, been the voice for those without a voice? Have we provided the hand down to embrace and lift up the weak and vulnerable?

You may have heard a preacher say, "If God spares America, He must apologize to Sodom and Gomorrah." God never needs to apologize for anything that He has done since He always does what is right. And He alone always knows the right response. But we are spared by His mercy, not our righteousness.

Revelation 19 follows the violent overthrow of Babylon. After God avenges innocent blood and claims His ultimate rule over the earth, the congregation's voice seems to John like "the roar of many waters and like the sound of mighty peals of thunder, crying out, 'Hallelujah!'" (v. 6).

The volume of praise becomes a crescendo as heaven reverberates and the worship leader modulates to a higher pitch. "Salvation and glory and power belong to our God, for his judgments are true and just; for he has judged the great prostitute who corrupted the earth with her immorality, and has avenged on her the blood of his servants. . . . Hallelujah! The smoke from her goes up forever and ever" (Rev. 19:1–3).

Does singing "hallelujah" sound like a strange response to the complete annihilation of a civilization? If so, perhaps we need to reevaluate our philosophy of worship. Praise is the right response to both God's kindness and His severity. For what He gives and what He takes away.

If perchance the image of a lion has not already been clear at this point in the Revelation, consider this description of Jesus Christ in Revelation 19:11–16:

Does singing "hallelujah" sound like a strange response to the complete annihilation of a civilization? If so, perhaps we need to reevaluate our philosophy of worship.

Then I saw heaven opened, and behold, a white horse! The one sitting on it is called Faithful and True, and in righteousness he judges and makes war. His eyes are like a flame of fire, and on his head are many diadems, and he has a name written that no one knows but himself. He is clothed in a robe dipped in blood, and the name by which he is called is The Word of God. And the armies of heaven, arrayed in fine linen, white and pure, were following him on white horses. From his mouth comes a sharp sword with which to strike down the nations, and he will rule them with a rod of iron. He will tread the winepress of the fury of the wrath of God the Almighty. On his robe and on his thigh he has a name written, King of kings and Lord of lords.

That intimidating description of a mighty military king is not from the older testament. This is our Jesus. This is the same Jesus we sang about when I was a child, "Jesus loves me, this I know."

I realize that much of Revelation uses symbolic language to describe reality. Without trying to interpret the above symbols, we can conclude that Jesus Christ, the Lion of Judah, is severe. He is sovereign. Repeating titles such as "King of kings" was the Hebrew way to emphasize this King is the greatest of all. No other ruler can compete with Jesus. He is in a category all by Himself.

So I wonder, is this picture in my "Jesus album" along with the handsome shepherd holding the lamb close to His chest? Is the lion king there beside the picture of Jesus cuddling little babies? Or have I deleted the Lion of Judah from my album? Do I even recognize this Jesus who will someday tread the winepress of the wrath of God? Do I claim Him? When did I last hear about this roaring lion in a sermon?

This fearsome image, however, is not the last picture of Jesus in Revelation. In the final chapter we will meet Him up close and personal and receive an invitation to enjoy His presence forever and to taste and discover the Lord is good.

That will not be the end. It will be the beginning of everything.

Thus far in this book, we have tried to follow a fairly logical progression, but there is an apparent challenge to God's kindness that we must now consider.

6

Is God Unfair?

*The Lord passed before him and proclaimed, "The Lord,
The Lord, a God merciful and gracious, slow to anger, and
abounding in steadfast love and faithfulness, keeping steadfast
love for thousands, forgiving iniquity and transgression
and sin, but who will by no means clear the guilty, visiting
the iniquity of the fathers on the children and the children's
children, to the third and fourth generation."*

Exodus 34:6–7

"Houston, we have a problem!"

Those gripping words spoken by Tom Hanks became the
tagline for the movie *Apollo 13*. It was the moment when a
well-executed space flight suddenly became a cliffhanger.

I hope our study about God's kindness and severity has
been an enlightening journey. Now we must address a potential problem. How can God be good if He punishes innocent
children for their parents' sin? How is that just? Every nerve in
our body recoils against something so unfair. We can't simply
ignore those troubling words in the book of Exodus. Whether
we like them or not, they form part of God's self-disclosure in
Scripture.

Remember the saying, "let sleeping dogs lie"? What should
we do when the dogs are wide awake and growling? What do

we do when the dilemma demands an answer?

In the passage quoted at the beginning of this chapter, God introduced Himself to Moses as Someone who is "merciful and gracious, slow to anger, and abounding in steadfast love and faithfulness, keeping steadfast love for thousands, forgiving iniquity and transgressions and sin . . ."

Yes! Who wouldn't admire and fall in love with this God?

But there is more to the story, isn't there? God is also holy and will not excuse our disobedience. He is not a doting grandpa with a limp handing out peppermints, but a powerful and righteous Judge who always carries out the appropriate sentence on the guilty.

I can live with *that* truth as well, and I can love that kind of God.

In fact, I wouldn't want a God who is fickle and capricious or who has a double standard when it comes to discipline. God doesn't play favorites in His courtroom. He will not be manipulated or bribed. There will be a final judgment day. Those who abuse the innocent will not receive a free pass, and really, *isn't that the way we want it?*

Even when we love someone, we still become angry when they make choices that threaten to ruin themselves or harm others. You have no doubt seen this dynamic at work among your own family or close friends. We all have. Tim Keller writes, "God's wrath flows from his love and delight in his creation. He is angry at evil and injustice because it is destroying peace and integrity."[1]

I realize the next example will date me, but I ask you to hang in there. Ed Ames released the popular song "Who Will Answer?" in 1967. The song described the turbulent era of the 1960s and '70s in American history. *Billboard* magazine described the song as expressing "the urgent feelings of our times and deal[ing] with such meaningful subjects as nuclear war, apathy, religious discontent and the underlying confusion of today's generation."[2] The lyrics reflect a universal desire for justice. Each of the six verses ends with the question, "Who will answer?"

The third verse describes a young soldier in Vietnam who will never hold his child, followed by the haunting question, "Who will answer?"

Another verse describes a "spreading mushroom tree"—an atomic bomb. Apparently someone pushed the "Red Button." Again, "Who will answer?"

The final verse drives home the point that we all want to know that someone has the final answer. The song concludes with three powerful words: "Hallelujah! Hallelujah! Hallelujah!"[3] I remember at the time being a little amazed that this secular song demanding an answer to the injustices in our world concluded with a threefold "Hallelujah" or "Praise the Lord!" Indeed, Someone has the answer.

As much as we appreciate God's self-disclosure to Moses, one troubling question remains: How can God be both loving and just if He punishes children for the sins of their parents and grandparents? To put it another way, does God actually punish children and grandchildren for something their parents have done? I don't claim to have all the answers—or even the best answer—but I want to take the opportunity to share several case studies from Scripture to help solve the dilemma.

Before we dig into the case studies, we must first consider the word translated *visit* in the ESV, NASB, and KJV—translated as *punish* in the NIV. I believe the NIV has made a poor translation. The Hebrew root word appears more than three hundred times in the older testament and can mean to visit someone or to carry out punishment upon someone, depending

GOD IN HIS OWN IMAGE

on the context. However, several Hebrew words for "punishment" could have been used to teach that God will punish innocent children, and none of those terms were used in this text. The word *visit* suggests the sin of a parent may have negative consequences resulting in collateral damage on innocent children. Perhaps the New English Translation is most clear: "But he by no means leaves the guilty unpunished, *responding to the transgression of fathers* by dealing with children and children's children, to the third and fourth generation" (emphasis mine).

Case Study #1: Before the Ink Could Dry

The First Giving of the Ten Commandments at Mount Sinai—Act 1

Exodus 20:5–6 is the first time in Scripture God promises to "visit" the sins of the parent on the children, and it's important to consider the context in which these seemingly unfair words came from the mouth of God. Before the dust had settled from chiseling out the Ten Commandments, before the proverbial ink had even dried, the first two laws were already being broken at the bottom of the mountain. After Moses had received the Commandments, he began his descent filled with anticipation of leading the nation in a grand ceremony consummating their covenant with God.

It didn't happen.

Brother Aaron, bowing to the demands of the restless Israelites, had forged a golden calf, proclaiming, "Tomorrow shall be a feast to the LORD." That sounded very noble. After all, what could be wrong with declaring a national day of thanksgiving?

The morning broke clear and the people brought offerings to present to the God who had delivered them from Egypt. But spiritual worship soon turned into a way-over-the-top sensual orgy. Note God's response in Exodus 32:7–8:

> And the Lord said to Moses, "Go down, for your people, whom you brought up out of the land of Egypt, have corrupted themselves. . . . They have made for themselves a golden calf and have worshiped it and sacrificed to it and said, 'These are your gods, O Israel, who brought you up out of the land of Egypt!'"

God called the Israelites "a stiff-necked people" and declared, "Now therefore let me alone, that *my wrath may burn hot against them and I may consume them*, in order that I may make a great nation of you" (Ex. 32:9–10, emphasis mine).

The phrase, "My wrath may burn hot against them and I may consume them," certainly connotes severe anger. We must not isolate this threat from the context of giving the Commandments. The first four commands in Exodus 20:1–11 deal with who God is and how He is to be treated.

Command #1: "You shall have *no other gods before me*" (v. 3). Period! No exceptions!

Command #2: "*You shall not make for yourself a carved image*, or any likeness of anything that is in heaven above, or that is in the earth beneath, or that is in the water under the earth. You shall not bow down to them or serve them, *for I the Lord your God am a jealous God, visiting the iniquity of the fathers on the children to the third and fourth generation* of those who hate me, but showing steadfast love to thousands of those who love me and keep my commandments" (vv. 4–5, emphasis mine).

The next two commands require proper respect for God's name and His holy Sabbath. To trivialize God's name is to dishonor His character and His person. Pretty serious stuff, wouldn't you say?

Since this is the first time God makes the statement about visiting sin on the children, it's important to note that the context deals specifically with idolatry. In fact, God's threat to discipline the children and grandchildren is part of a longer sentence warning against idolatry, "You shall not bow down to them or serve them, for I the LORD your God am *a jealous God, visiting the iniquity* of the fathers on the children . . ."

God's jealousy, unlike ours, is not the result of insecurity or a need to control somebody. His jealousy is not suspicious but demands exclusive devotion.

Two words, *jealous* and *visiting*, provide a key to resolving the paradox of whether God punishes children for something their parents did. We have already considered the word *visit* above.

God's jealousy, unlike ours, is not the result of insecurity or a need to control somebody. His jealousy is not suspicious but demands exclusive devotion. In traditional marriage vows, we promise "to forsake all others" and to keep ourselves only for our spouse. A truly loving wife or husband will not tolerate their spouse sleeping around with others. And neither will God transfer His honor or glory to another.

When Israel pursued idols, God accused them of spiritual adultery. God expects and deserves our total commitment in response to His love. Consider the Great Shema in Deuteronomy 6:4, "You shall love the LORD your God with *all* your heart and with *all* your soul and with *all* your might." That is total commitment!

Passage after passage in the older testament underlines God's jealousy against idolatry.[4] In Isaiah 42:8 and 48:11 God makes it abundantly clear that He *will not* share His glory with another.

> **To ascribe God's glory to an idol is like looking at Leonardo da Vinci's *Mona Lisa* and saying, "A kindergarten kid could do better."**

God is God! He tolerates no competitors in the relationship. He is sovereign! For this reason, He will not and cannot permit us to transfer or ascribe His glory to a lesser being. To do so is more insulting than visiting the Sistine Chapel, seeing Michelangelo's frescoes on the ceiling, and saying something stupid like, "Oh, look! Somebody let their kids scribble on the ceiling!"

To ascribe God's glory to an idol is like looking at Leonardo da Vinci's *Mona Lisa* and saying, "A kindergarten kid could do better."

The Second Giving of the Commandments—Act 2

In Exodus 34:1–28, we have the account of the second chiseling out of the Commandments in stone, renewing the covenant between God and Israel. The covenant concludes with another warning against falling into the idolatry of the nations that Israel would replace in Canaan. They were to destroy every pagan altar and every idol, "for you shall worship no other god, for the LORD, whose name is Jealous, is a jealous God" (v. 14).

The Generation Crossing into the Promised Land—Act 3

The warning about visiting parents' sins on their children is repeated again in Deuteronomy 5:8–9 when the Commandments were given to the generation that had survived the forty-year wilderness trek. The title Deuteronomy means "Second Law." It is the *deutero* or the second time the *nomos* or Law had been given to Israel. And, once again, the warning about visiting the sin of the parents on their children appears immediately following warnings against idolatry. Why? Because God jealously guards His name and character.

What can we conclude after looking at these case studies? It's pretty clear, isn't it?

The warning about children suffering the consequences of their parents' sins is related specifically to idolatry. Idolatry is not insignificant; it is an insult and assault against the very nature of God to create something out of wood or metal or stone and call it "The Creator," or any other title rightly belonging to God alone.

Idolatry also influences the entire culture. Visit any polytheistic country such as India and witness the generational influences of idolatry. We can read about or watch movies about the Christian missionaries who penetrated pagan tribes such as the Huaorani people, formerly known as the Aucas in Ecuador. Prior to missionaries bringing the gospel to the Huaorani people—at the cost of the lives of five American martyrs—the Aucas worshiped natural phenomena, including the sun. Every little tribal group warred upon members of neighboring groups. It was reported that the most common cause of death was murder. Each little boy growing up in this culture adopted the same violent lifestyle; there was *always* a grudge to settle, resulting in endemic violence being passed from generation to generation.

The sin of the parents was passed on to their children.

And so was the consequence!

In Leviticus 26, God once again commanded the Israelites to make no idols or to worship them. This time God warned He would withhold rain until famine conditions brought them to near starvation. If the adults turned to idols, their children would suffer hunger and famine along with their parents. Since the fall, consequences have been built into the reality of the order of things. Our choices result in often-predictable consequences.

Unfortunately, Israel had a difficult time breaking their love affair with idols. Perhaps a little bit of Egypt, besides gold jewelry, clung to them after the exodus. The pagan culture, including idolatry, was ingrained in their hearts.

God's prophets frequently called the nation of Israel back to their one true God and away from pagan idols, but every revival was followed by another relapse.

For example, Solomon, wise man that he was, foolishly made alliances with pagan kings and married foreign women who brought their foreign gods with them. Solomon's sinful choices would affect generations to come. The kingdom was divided and ten tribes were given to Jeroboam. Because Jeroboam feared the people would be influenced toward Rehoboam by worshiping at the temple in Jerusalem, he introduced an alternative religion involving worship of a golden calf. It doesn't take a genius to discover where that idea came from. That specific sin of Aaron returned to plague Israel again.

The blatant, nonstop sin of idolatry in the northern tribes eventually resulted in the Assyrian invasion and the forced resettlement for most of the population. The ten northern tribes lost both their national and racial identity, intermarrying with Gentiles and becoming known as the despised Samaritans in the newer testament.

Because Judah had the temple and a few righteous kings who led national revival movements, they survived longer than their northern brothers. Eventually, however, the sin of idolatry resulted in the Babylonian invasion and captivity. The parents and grandparents had pursued idolatry, and once again the children and grandchildren also paid a severe price in the exile.

In yet another graphic example of this same phenomenon, we read in Jeremiah 16:1–13 about the long-term, generational consequences of idolatry—and its addictive hold over the people. The prophet had consistently warned his nation that their idolatry would result in the invasion and exile to Babylon. Judah had crossed the line of no return. Jeremiah was even forbidden to marry or have children because of the coming invasion and horrific slaughter. Parents would soon grieve the death of their children. God said, "I have taken away my peace from this people, my steadfast love and mercy" (v. 5).

God also warned, "Behold, I will silence in this place, before your eyes and in your days, the voice of mirth and the voice of gladness, the voice of the bridegroom and the voice of the bride" (Jer. 16:9).

When Judah questioned why God was doing this, His response in Jeremiah 16:13 was, *"Because your fathers have forsaken me . . .* and have gone after other gods and have served and worshiped them, and have forsaken me and have not kept my law, and *because you have done worse than your fathers . . . therefore I will hurl you out of this land into a land that neither you nor your fathers have known"* (emphasis mine).

The sin of idolatry had a debilitating effect on an entire nation; figuratively speaking, it had become part of their shared DNA. Each successive generation became more comfortable with and more committed to worshiping gods made by their own hands. The result was devastating—the destruction of their nation and seventy years in exile. Seventy long years separated from their homes and the temple—and the nation never did return to its former prominence in the world. God punished parents and grandparents, but the children and grandchildren were not spared the severe consequences of their parents' sin.

When you think about it, how could it have been otherwise?

It has been said, "God's wrath is not a cranky explosion, but his settled opposition to the cancer of sin which is eating out the insides of the human race he loves with his whole being."[5]

Case Study #2: A Disastrous Wrong Turn

Numbers 14:17–35 describes one of the great turning points in the Bible. God had promised to travel with Israel and deliver them into the Promised Land. But the people grumbled about the lack of meat in their diet and criticized Moses.

God had been patient with them to this point. They were now a mere fifty miles from the borders of the Promised Land—a distance they could have covered in a week or two.

Instead, it ended up taking them *forty years.* This massive, tragic change in their destiny happened because of the deliberate choice not to trust God. Twelve Israelite leaders had explored Canaan, and they verified that it was a good land—even *very* good. But ten men focused on the perceived obstacles of walled cities peopled by giant warriors. Their bad report resulted in open rebellion against Moses and against God.

Elevating whining to a new art form, they wept aloud and complained, "Would that we had died in this wilderness! Why is the Lord bringing us into this land, to fall by the sword? Our wives and our little ones will become a prey. Would it not be better for us to go back to Egypt? . . . Let us choose a leader and go back to Egypt" (Num. 14:1–4).

After all God had done for them and after all the miracles in leaving Egypt—including parting the sea—they dared to question God's goodness and power. By threatening to choose another leader, they were rejecting God Himself!

Once again, God threatened to destroy the entire bunch of

rebels and start over with righteous Moses. Listen to Moses's prayer as he quotes the very words God had spoken on the mountain: "The LORD is slow to anger and abounding in steadfast love, forgiving iniquity and transgression, but he will by no means clear the guilty, *visiting the iniquity of the fathers on the children, to the third and the fourth generation.* Please pardon the iniquity of this people, according to the greatness of your steadfast love, just as you have forgiven this people, from Egypt until now" (Num. 14:18–26, emphasis mine). Moses is reminding God (as if God forgets) of His promises and of His character.

The stiff safety latch on His wrath restrained His anger and the nation was spared once again. But there was a severe price to pay. A journey that should have taken a couple of weeks became forty painful years. Every adult died who had accused God of bringing their children to die in the wilderness. The children were not directly punished for their parents' sin, but did they suffer collateral damage in their long, futile trek through the wasteland? Of course they did.

Case Study #3: Stolen Treasures

Another seemingly extreme example of God punishing children for a father's sin is the story of Achan in Joshua 7:10–19. Achan, an Israeli soldier who fought in the overwhelming victory over Jericho, had collected valuable souvenirs and hid them in his tent. However, everything in Jericho had been totally devoted to God and nobody was to claim any booty for themselves. Achan's sin resulted in defeat in the battle against Ai, costing the lives of thirty-six of his comrades.

Trusting God to reveal the guilty person, Joshua began to eliminate, by lot, tribes and family groups who were innocent. Achan's sin was ultimately exposed and he and his immediate family were stoned to death and their bodies burned. We can understand capital punishment being inflicted on Achan—the one who brought such grief upon Israel. But why kill his wife and kids? Bible scholars agree that Achan could not have hidden the items under his tent without the family knowing or seeing.

Any one of them, including Achan, could have come forward to confess the crime at any point during the process of elimination as the finger began to point more and more toward them. Every member of Achan's family was complicit in the crime and the cover-up.

Achan knew, going into the battle against Jericho, both the command against and the consequence for taking anything dedicated to God. This was especially true about taking a Canaanite idol. This severe penalty upon Achan's family had already been determined when Israel was still on the other side of the Jordan River when they publicly entered into a covenant with God. Moses, now pushing 120 years old, shared both the blessings and the curses within the covenant. God had promised to drive out the Canaanites, but Moses also specifically commanded the Israelites in Deuteronomy 7:25–26 to burn every Canaanite carved image and to not *"bring an abominable thing into your house and become devoted to destruction like it"* (emphasis mine). Achan was part of the congregation that heard the warning and had verbally promised to obey or suffer death along with his family. Joshua simply enforced the existing law by pronouncing the devastating sentence on Achan and his family.

Achan's sin was far greater than hiding some forbidden booty under his tent. He had caused God's blessing to be lifted from the Israelite army, resulting in disaster at Ai. Furthermore, if this one sin had gone unchecked, it would have surely opened the door for more sin—possibly keeping Israel from experiencing their destiny in the Promised Land.

Case Study #4: Lying to the Holy Spirit

A similar situation occurred in the fifth chapter of the book of Acts, at the dawn of the church of Jesus Christ. Ananias and Sapphira lied to the Lord and to church leaders at a very crucial moment in the church's history. Sin unchecked at this point in the infant church would have had disastrous effects. It must have been a very memorable church service—two deaths and two burials. But after this shocking incident, the membership had been put on notice: God would not and will not ignore sin. A little leaven would infect the whole batch.

Think of sin as a deadly virus or a cancer cell and the human race as a living organism. Sin, like a malignant cell, spreads and destroys surrounding tissue.

Think of sin as a deadly virus or a cancer cell and the human race as a living organism. Sin, like a malignant cell, spreads and destroys surrounding tissue. Sin and its consequences may be transmitted from generation to generation. A promiscuous parent may contract the HIV virus and a baby suffers. A pregnant woman chooses to use drugs and a meth baby is born. A negligent father chooses not to work or abuses alcohol and his family lives in poverty. Parents divorce and children are wounded. Some divorces may be justified. Nevertheless, all divorces leave collateral damage and unanticipated consequences.

J. D. Vance, a product of a very dysfunctional family, shares how generational sins have affected him and his family. Vance writes in his book, *Hillbilly Elegy,* how everyday occurrences in his family affected him and his siblings. Psychologists call these occurrences "adverse childhood experiences" or ACEs. The trauma may not be physical but includes any of the following events or feelings.[6]

- being sworn at, insulted, or humiliated by parents
- being pushed, grabbed, or having something thrown at you
- feeling that your family didn't support each other
- having parents who were separated or divorced
- living with an alcoholic or a drug user
- living with someone who was depressed or attempted suicide
- watching a loved one be physically abused

Even in situations such as these, however, there is still hope. Vance's grandmother was raised in rural Kentucky in a home adversely affected by generations of alcohol abuse as well as verbal and physical abuse. Moving to Ohio introduced them into a new culture with opportunities for employment and social advancement, but the turbulent relationships between mother and daughter continued, often creating very unsafe environments for J. D. and his sister. The abuse and neglect of J. D.'s mother eventually resulted in him being reared by his grandmother—the only stable adult in his life at the time. Yet her parenting skills were very dysfunctional too.

J. D. was fortunate to break the dysfunctional generational cycle. He eventually attended Ohio State University and received a postgraduate degree from Yale. Even so, he admits he is still adversely affected at times by his childhood experiences.

Families are not trapped in an endless cycle of sin and consequences, because the chain can be broken at any point in time through the amazing power of the gospel. Mary and I have been foster parents for three precious young people who have been dealt a bad deck of cards by others' choices. It is our prayer that we, by the grace of God, may have helped them break the cycle of destructive generational consequences.

I teach at the Shepherd's House, a local faith-based recovery ministry in Bend, and am personally involved with several of the men. Their stories, almost without exception, are the same. Their fathers, sometimes their mothers, were alcoholics and often abusive or absent. Many are the second or third generation who struggle with chemical dependency. I have come to love these men who have been hurt by the choices of their parents as much as by their own choices.

One of the men, Frankie (he now prefers to be called Frank), calls me Pops. His story ought to be in print, for it is the story of the incomparable power of God to break the chains of sin. Frank may have lived as much of his adult life in prison as out, but today he is a new man whose chains have been broken. Recently over breakfast at IHOP, Frank prayed before the meal. His prayer blew me away. It also humbled me. He prayed for the chefs and the server who brought the food to our table. (He was unaware she had returned with Tabasco sauce and was standing beside our booth.) His prayer was that God would somehow reveal Himself to her that day and that she would come to know Jesus. I have never prayed for the chef in a restaurant. I have never thought to pray for the servers to come to faith in Christ that day. Frank claims I have had an impact on his life, but I confess he has had a great effect on me.

Case Study #5: Generational Sour Grapes

In Jeremiah 31:29 and Ezekiel 18:2, we encounter this puzzling metaphor: "*The fathers have eaten sour grapes, and the children's teeth will be set on edge."* In that day and time, it was a familiar proverb that suggested children paid for their parents' sins.

Have you ever bitten into a chokecherry? Possibly not, unless you happened to grow up in the sand hill country of western Nebraska. Tasting a chokecherry for the first time (or the fiftieth) is a unique experience, as you might deduce from its name. It is so tart, so incredibly sour, that your mouth puckers and even your teeth react.

This ancient proverb about biting sour grapes illustrated a false assumption that children would be punished if the father sinned. Both Jeremiah and Ezekiel debunk the proverb.

Jeremiah 31:30 clearly states that *"Everyone shall die for his own iniquity. Each man who eats sour grapes, his teeth shall be set on edge"* (emphasis mine).

The Bible clearly teaches that God, because He is fair and just, will not punish innocent people for the willful sin of another person.

Ezekiel 18:1–4, 30 also drives home the truth that God does not punish children for something their parents did:

> The word of the LORD came to me: "What do you mean by repeating this proverb concerning the land of Israel, 'The fathers have eaten sour grapes, and the children's teeth are set on edge'? As I live, declares the Lord GOD, this proverb shall no more be used by you in Israel. Behold, all souls are mine; the soul of the father as well as the soul of the son is mine: *the soul who sins shall die."* ... *"I will judge ... every one according to his ways."* (emphasis mine)

The Bible clearly teaches that God, because He is fair and just, will not punish innocent people for the willful sin of another person. If children turn away from imitating their parents' sin, they will not be punished. History, however, is replete with examples of innocent people becoming collateral damage because of the sin of another highly influential person—be it a sibling, a parent, a friend, or a political leader. Our decisions can have an impact on others. As the apostle Paul put it, "Bad company corrupts good character" (1 Cor. 15:33 NIV).

The problem is not in the nature of God but in the nature of sin.

We are coming to the end of our study about God's kindness and severity. I have tried to present both attributes in balance. Now, let us consider God's offer to taste and see how sweet it is to know Him. I will also share about my experience of discovering God's grace and unconditional love.

7

Taste and See

Oh, taste and see that the LORD is good!
Blessed is the man who takes refuge in him!

Psalm 34:8

"Come to me, all who labor and are heavy laden, and I will
give you rest. Take my yoke upon you, and learn from me, for I
am gentle and lowly in heart, and you will find rest for your
souls. For my yoke is easy, and my burden is light."

Matthew 11:28–30

You have to wonder how certain expressions crept into our language. I think of the phrase, "The proof is in the pudding." What in the world does that mean? According to language expert Ben Zimmer, the expression is actually a new twist on a very old proverb. The original wording stated, "The proof of the pudding is in the eating." Which means, of course, you have to taste a given food before you know whether it's good or not.[1]

When my wife and I visit a favorite restaurant, I like to order something I've never had before. Mary, on the other hand, searches for a familiar item on the menu—something she *knows* she likes—and sticks with it. (Over and over again.)

Why does she do that? Because she doesn't want to "go home disappointed." I, on the other hand, may certainly go home disappointed, but I will be wiser. I enjoy the challenge of discovering something new. And more often than not, I like it.

It's interesting to me that God Himself offers a "proof-is-in-the-pudding" challenge when it comes to knowing Him. In Psalm 34:8 we read, "Oh, taste and see that the LORD is good! Blessed is the man who takes refuge in him!" *The Message* paraphrase renders the verse like this: "Open your mouth and taste, open your eyes and see—how good God is. Blessed are you who run to him."

Throughout these pages, I have been trying to remind myself and you that God's flavor—what He tastes like—has elements of both kindness and severity. Psalm 34:8, however, suggests to me that after we have tasted both sides of His nature—His gracious kindness and His fearsome severity—we will quickly conclude He is good.

"Open your mouth and taste . . . open your eyes and see."

If my emphasis in this book has been more upon God's sterner attributes, it's because very few people talk about them anymore. God's wrath doesn't sound as appealing on the menu. Maybe so, but God's attributes aren't buffet items in a cafeteria line. We can't pick and choose which aspects of His character we like, rejecting those that make us uncomfortable or that we find difficult to explain.

> **We can't pick and choose which aspects of His character we like, rejecting those that make us uncomfortable or that we find difficult to explain.**

That, my friend, would be creating a "god" in our own image.

Which is another way of saying *idolatry*.

God only offers the "full meal deal." He invites us to taste who He is—all that He is—and discover for ourselves that He is truly good. All the way and all the time.

Yes, we may struggle when we hear about God's severity and wonder how our heavenly Father can be both kind and also filled with fury. One thing however, is absolutely certain. In the Bible there is one God. There aren't two.

God 2.0?

Jesus is not God 2.0. He isn't a revised version of the deity with a friendlier face and a quaint Galilean accent. Jesus is the Good Shepherd who lays down His life for the sheep and the Lion that picks up the sword and wreaks vengeance. But how, then, does God know "which hat to wear" at any given moment?

When I was a student at Western Seminary in Portland, Oregon, as well as full-time pastor of Powellhurst Baptist Church, I was also a husband and a father of two boys. Looking back now, I shake my head. What hard years! I was always feeling conflicted. If I was studying for my Hebrew literature classes, I heard this small voice saying, *"You ought to be preparing the sermon because it's Friday and Sunday's coming."* But if I was preparing a sermon, that accusing voice whispered, *"Shame on you! You should be out playing with your sons or taking your wife to a movie."*

My life had become too complex. I had too many hats to wear. Oh yes, we survived. I received my degree, the church didn't fall apart, and I still had time to be with my wife and kids. Did I attempt too much? In 20/20 hindsight, yes I did. But God was gracious and kind to me and my family, in spite of some ill-considered decisions.

The July/August 2017 edition of *Christianity Today* featured an article by Derek Rishmawy titled, "Life Is Complex.

God Is Not."[2] That title drew me like a magnet; I had to read it. As an illustration, the author describes a scene from *The Crown*, a celebrated Netflix miniseries about Queen Elizabeth's ascension to the throne and her early reign.

When Elizabeth became queen, she discovered that her responsibilities as monarch frequently conflicted with her roles as sister, mother, and wife. Her life became exceedingly complex at times, but one reality kept her on track: her highest priority was to act as queen of the United Kingdom, no matter how difficult that might be and no matter who might be disappointed with her.

God has many roles in Scripture. The same is true of Jesus, as we have already seen. Jesus is Lion and Lamb, Shepherd and Priest, Savior and King. In the book of Revelation, He is the quality control inspector of the churches, while He is also the husband of His bride, the church. In the Gospels, Jesus is the babe in the manger and the man on the cross. In the concluding chapters of Revelation, He is the severe judge and military general, mounted on a white warhorse.

He has many roles, but He never changes. He is the same yesterday, today, and forever.

He has many roles, but He never changes. He is "the same yesterday and today and forever" (Heb. 13:8).

Even in His judgment there is love, and in His love we may find stern discipline. "Those whom I love, I reprove and discipline, so be zealous and repent." Both Revelation 3:19 and Hebrews 12:4–6 support the above statement.

Rishmawy comments, "To say God is 'simple' isn't to say he's easily understood or lacks mystery. It is to say he is not complex." God, in other words, is "simply himself in all that he does. . . . In order to be the Father, God never had to take off the crown."[3]

With these things in mind, let's take another quick look at God's self-disclosure in Exodus 34.

A Close Encounter

Moses boldly asked—really, almost demanded—"Please show me your glory" (Ex. 33:18).

God responded, "I will make all my goodness pass before you and will proclaim before you my name 'The LORD.'... But you cannot see my face, for *man shall not see me and live*" (vv. 19–20, emphasis mine). If that wasn't intimidating enough, don't forget Moses's previous encounters with God. At the burning bush God warned, "Take off your shoes, for this is holy ground" (see Ex. 3:5). While on the way to Egypt, God was prepared to kill Moses for failing to circumcise his sons. God also warned that anybody who dared to approach the mountain, man or beast, would perish.

Those encounters should be sufficient to put us on alert as we revisit Exodus 34. The day finally arrived; Moses was eagerly waiting (but with a good bit of apprehension) when

> the LORD descended in the cloud and stood with him there, and proclaimed the name of the LORD. The LORD passed before him and proclaimed, "The LORD, the LORD, a God merciful and gracious, slow to anger, and abounding in steadfast love and faithfulness, keeping steadfast love for thousands, forgiving iniquity and transgression and sin, but who will by no means clear the guilty, visiting the iniquity of the fathers on the children and the children's children, to the third and fourth generation." (Ex. 34:5–7)

Since that is how God wants to be known, how shall we relate to Him? Moses's first response to the right one; he "quickly bowed his head toward the earth and worshiped" (Exodus 34:8–9). Good idea, don't you agree?

God also promised to enter into a covenant with Israel and to do marvelous things for them that had never been seen before.

Moses lingered on the mountain forty days in the presence of God receiving the first edition of the Commandments and detailed instructions for constructing the tabernacle. Everything in and about the tabernacle was spectacular, lavish with fine workmanship and the gleam of gold. Even the priestly garment for Aaron was designed "for glory and beauty" according to Exodus 28:2. The robe with its rich colors of gold, blue, purple, and scarlet made of finely twisted linen was adorned with precious stones including a diamond.

But the most important feature was not the gold or the eye-pleasing work of skilled artisans. All that creativity and beauty paled when "the cloud covered the tent of meeting, and the glory of the LORD filled the tabernacle. And Moses was not able to enter the tent of meeting because the cloud settled on it, and the glory of the LORD filled the tabernacle" (Ex. 40:34–35).

> Israel discovered a personal God who loved them and watched over them day and night like a compassionate father. This is our God today!

No Hollywood special effects studio equipped with supercomputers could begin to portray the wonder, fear, and beauty of that moment. Think of it! The Almighty Creator of the universe had actually come to live among His people! Because God had revealed Himself to them, Israel discovered a personal God who loved them and watched over them day and night like a compassionate father. This is our God today!

God seeks a relationship with us as He did with Adam and Eve and Abraham and Moses. I am convinced that the deeper our relationship with God grows, the less we will be driven by fear and the more we will be drawn by His love and His kindness. Remember the quote from G. Campbell Morgan? "The reason for man's fear of God is not in God; it is in man. The men who have known God best have had the least fear of him and have exulted in their conversation concerning him and their relation to him. . . . God calling Adam is not the call of a policeman, it is the wail of a father . . . of God in the presence of human sin."[4]

I am grateful that I no longer live under those man-made rules of my childhood church and my Cosmic Cop image of God. Sometimes I wonder if I may be the only young person from that church of my youth who still loves Jesus. Sadly, most have rejected Christ because of the legalism and hypocrisy. They turned their backs on a kind and gracious God because they never heard or saw evidence of Him.

Perhaps the best thing that happened to me was when my dad resigned from the ministry during my sophomore year of high school. I was then free to try a different fellowship and began attending Grace Baptist Church in Sidney, Nebraska. Pastor Greene wasn't a world-class preacher, but he was kind and gracious, as was his wife, who taught the high school class. At Grace Baptist I really did discover grace, and my entire life began to change. It was like a block of ice melting inside my soul.

Without that intervention, without making that change, I am convinced I would have never become a pastor—and might not even be a believer today.

While I sat under the loving ministry of Pastor and Mrs.

Greene, Jesus became a real person to me. Eventually I felt the call into the ministry and chose to attend Moody Bible Institute. Happily, I experienced grace at Moody, too. I loved studying the Bible in those years and learning more about God—as I do to this day.

God isn't a specimen on a biology lab table, He is a person. He wants us to enter into a relationship with Him, not just know about Him.

When I mention that I enjoyed learning about God, it could almost sound like our high school biology lab when we dissected earthworms and frogs. Some of my lab partners didn't enjoy cutting up a pickled worm, but it was necessary to pass the course. God, however, isn't a specimen on a biology lab table. He is a person. He wants us to enter into a relationship with Him, not just know about Him.

How Do I Enjoy God?

Maybe you've heard these words from the Westminster Shorter Catechism: "The chief end [purpose] of man is to glorify God and to enjoy him forever."[5]

I suspect everyone feels comfortable with the phrase "to glorify God."

But to *enjoy* Him?

As a young person from a legalistic church the phrase would have sounded strange to me—maybe even borderline blasphemous. I knew about God's holiness and wrath. I knew about the Cosmic Cop who watched my every step. But who could feel close to such a God? And who in the world could "enjoy" Him?

Listen to a very early biblical description of a man who truly enjoyed God. In Genesis 5:23–24, we read: "Thus all the days of Enoch were 365 years. Enoch walked with God, and he was not, for God took him."

When I read that sentence, I imagine an old man who really looked forward to His daily walks with God. *The Message* paraphrase says he "walked steadily with God" (Gen. 5:22). Adding up the numbers of Enoch's life, I like to imagine that God surprised him on his 365th birthday as they took a short-cut directly to heaven.

Can't you just visualize it? The Lord says to Enoch, "This way, My friend."

"Yes, Lord, but . . . I don't recognize this path. Where are we going?"

"We've walked so far, Enoch. Why don't you just come on home with Me?"

Much later in Scripture, David is described as "a man after God's own heart." He even wrote Psalm 27 expressing his joy in knowing God:

> One thing have I asked of the LORD,
>   that will I seek after:
> that I may dwell in the house of the LORD
>   all the days of my life,
> to gaze on the beauty of the LORD
>   and to inquire in his temple.

A. W. Tozer said, "[David's] psalms ring with the cry of the seeker and the glad shout of the finder."[6] Sometimes David felt like a prospector searching for gold, in this case God, but he is also the man who has discovered the mother lode and shouts "Eureka!"

Relationships are never static but are meant to grow deeper. After celebrating fifty-two years of marriage, I have come to know Mary more intimately. Certainly, I appreciate all the things she does to please me, but I'm not talking about appreciating what Mary *does*. I just flat out enjoy her more than ever. When I am away from her, I can't wait to return to her, and I really can't imagine life without her.

Once again we have to ask, *How can finite and fallen human beings like ourselves ever understand Someone so infinite and so holy?* That thought is very similar to the question Zophar asked in the ancient book of Job: "Can you fathom the mysteries of God? Can you probe the limits of the Almighty? They are higher than the heavens above—what can you do? They are deeper than the depths below—what can you know? Their measure is longer than the earth and wider than the sea" (Job 11:7–9 NIV).

I love Zophar's word *fathom*. To fathom something means to get to the bottom of it. A fathom is also a maritime measurement equaling approximately six feet. We may, with modern technology, be able to measure or fathom the depths of the oceans, but we can never fathom or get to the bottom of all there is to know about God.

Not even close.

He is fathomless. He is beyond comprehension. God is unlike anything we know or understand. That was also the opinion of several biblical authors:

His greatness no one can fathom. (Ps. 145:3 NIV)

His understanding no one can fathom. (Is. 40:28 NIV)

How unsearchable are his judgments and how inscrutable his ways! (Rom. 11:33)

Treasure Hunt

If God really wants us to know Him, why doesn't He just fully reveal Himself to us? Why doesn't Jesus simply appear in a vision—right now, in the room where you're sitting? Why doesn't He invite us to "touch Me and see" as He did with Thomas in the upper room (see John 20:24–29)? A. W. Tozer insightfully observes, "To have found God and still to pursue Him is the soul's paradox of love."[7]

Tozer's comment reminds me of our grandchildren visiting us at Christmas when they were small. Mary always planned a treasure hunt for them. The kids were the magi searching for clues to lead them to the young child in Bethlehem. At each designated spot—perhaps the clothes dryer, or the second shelf in the linen closet—they discovered a treasure and another clue leading them to the next hidden cache. The oohs and ahs at each new discovery were rewarding, but they weren't satisfied to stop after finding the first treasure.

The joy and excitement wasn't in simply adding another item to their gift bags. The excitement was in the search itself! The fun was in figuring out each clue and racing breathlessly to the next destination. So it is with God and with Jesus. We find reward and joy in each new discovery, but each eureka moment only increases our appetite to search more deeply.

Knowing God is like drinking deeply from the freshest, coolest, and sweetest spring on earth, wiping your mouth, and immediately desiring another drink.

Knowing God is like drinking deeply from the freshest, coolest, and sweetest spring on earth, wiping your mouth, and immediately desiring another drink. Your thirst is quenched but never quenched. Satisfied but never satisfied.

It's like having a passion for hiking in the mountains. The more beauty I discover, the more I want to search for another wildflower or another breathtaking view.

Or let me try it another way. The marriage ceremony isn't the end of courtship. It's the very beginning of growing more intimate. I thought I knew Mary when I proposed on the shore of Lake Michigan, and I thought I knew her well on our silver anniversary. But today I smile as I realize how little I really knew or appreciated Mary back then. The more I learn about her, the more I want to know her.

I'm a student at heart, and dearly love to study and interpret the Bible. After decades of studying to prepare sermons, I continue to discover hidden nuggets just below the surface of the written page. There's no end to them, and every new discovery is as amazing as the last.

Now, if discovering golden nuggets on paper makes me want to keep searching for more, how much greater the passion to know God! I am grateful that my spiritual journey did not end back there in my childhood church when God was the Cosmic Cop or the severe father. Today He is so much more attractive and so much more personal. I realize the search has just begun, because deep veins of gold still wait to be discovered.

My Journey

I once believed God doesn't care *where* you serve, but rather about *why* you serve. I still believe the why, your essential motivation, is vital. But my story is filled with examples of God opening and closing doors to surprise me with something better than I had been seeking. I will share just three examples.

I was raised on a wheat farm in the Panhandle of Nebraska

and am an introvert. I never raised my hand in the classroom and avoided giving oral reports or speeches. I would ace the written requirements and refuse the oral. So when I sensed (to my great surprise) God calling me into ministry, it took two years before I had the courage to apply to Moody Bible Institute. I feared having to take speech and homiletic courses. While at Moody when I listened to tapes of myself preaching in homiletic classes I would say, *God, I can't do this. You have the wrong man.*

After completing my undergrad degree at Moody, I applied for a job at North Electric in Galion, Ohio, where we were living. Mary was pregnant, and I needed work badly. The personnel manager looked at my application and noticed I had graduated from Moody. She was convinced it was a sign from God, because she was serving on a pastoral search committee for her small country church. They had just contacted Moody to see if any alumni might apply for the position. She never talked about a job at the factory but couldn't stop talking about their little church's need for a pastor.

I had planned to apply to Dallas Seminary within a year and wasn't interested in a pastorate right then. After six months, however, God convinced us His plan was for me to pastor Pulaskiville Community Church rather than go to seminary. God wasn't slow; I was just stubborn.

At Pulaskiville, I learned to preach and teach and watch God work in the congregation. The little church of forty-five began to grow until more than two hundred attended. Those seven and a half years in a country church prepared me for seminary. In the fall of 2016, we visited Ohio and met with several friends from the church. I was humbled to hear person after person share how God had used me to introduce them to Christ and to help them grow.

God's plan for me was perfect. In that day and in that time, little Pulaskiville was the center of the universe for Mary and me. In that season of life, those years in the country church were better for me than a hundred years in seminary.

A decade later, while I was attending Western Seminary in Portland, a professor placed my name as a pastoral candidate at Powellhurst Baptist Church. I had planned to work half-time at UPS and finish seminary in three years. God, however, planned for us to pastor a dying church and watch Him resurrect it. We enjoyed thirteen amazing years at Powellhurst, and I was prepared to remain there for another thirteen.

I had declined several requests to candidate at different churches. First Baptist Church in Bend was searching for a pastor and requested my résumé. I said no to them (and to God) for several months. Every time I gave God a reason I couldn't go to Bend, He removed my excuse in a dramatic way.

The final reason I refused to go to Bend was Lance (not his real name), a man whose father had sexually abused him and abandoned the family. His stepfather repeated the same sins. Lance fought depression and trusted nobody. I had the privilege of sharing the gospel with Lance and his wife one day. It was like a light came on as Lance learned about someone who loved him and would never abandon him. He became a passionate follower of Jesus. We were the same age, but I became his father figure. I told God one Saturday morning, "I can't go to Bend because it would be one more person who had abandoned Lance."

The following morning Lance asked to meet with me between church services. He looked into my face and said, "I hear there is a church in Bend that wants you to be their pastor. I don't want you to go, but God sent me here to release you."

I swear those were his very words.

I had my plan; God's plan was better. He gives the best to

those who leave the choice to Him. We enjoyed twenty-four years serving First Baptist, now Foundry Church, and are still welcome there as members.

I am a living testimony that the greatest privilege in life is to know God and to enjoy Him now and forever! The lyrics of an old gospel song say it well: "The longer I serve Him, the sweeter He grows."[8]

Honoring the God Who Loves Us

My wife has a neat saying she picked up years ago: "I'm drinking from a saucer because my cup overflows." Didn't David say something like that?

> You prepare a table before me
>   in the presence of my enemies;
> you anoint my head with oil;
>   my cup overflows.
> Surely goodness and mercy shall follow me
>   all the days of my life,
> and I shall dwell in the house of the LORD
>   forever. (Ps. 23:5–6)

David felt like a child enjoying an extravagant feast. His plate was filled, and servants refilled his cup again and again. But David looked beyond his present circumstances. He knew there was something beyond savoring God's goodness and mercy through the days of life. By faith, he clung to the conviction that he would one day live in God's own house, enjoying Him forever.

Consider another satisfied seeker. Saul of Tarsus had grown up as the very definition of a religious legalist. Filled with anger and hatred toward what he saw as a cult, Saul pressed forward on his deadly mission to stamp out Christians and this new sect. Suddenly the blinding "Light of the world" knocked him to the ground and a voice demanded, "Saul, Saul, why are you persecuting me?" Fearing for his life he cried out, "Who are you, Lord?" Little did he realize that he was about to meet Jesus Christ and begin a relationship that would transform his life and ultimately lead to his death as a martyr.

The relationship that began on a dusty road grew more and more intimate. His name changed to Paul as part of his new identity in Christ. Once an avowed enemy of Jesus and persecutor of the followers of Christ, Paul now counted every other pursuit in life as worthless as a pile of manure compared to knowing Jesus. Listen to his words written from a Roman prison while facing the death squad: "I count everything [else] as a loss because of the surpassing worth of knowing Christ Jesus my Lord. . . . That I may know him and the power of his resurrection, and may share his sufferings, becoming like him in his death" (Phil. 3:8, 10).

Having met the Lord, Paul was forever changed. Here was a man who knew what it meant to know Christ and to enjoy Him forever. That is also our privilege today! The Jesus we meet in the newer testament is the same God who met Moses on the mountain. He desires a relationship with people like you and me—but that relationship will always be on His terms, not ours.

He is inexpressibly kind, yes.

He is also severe, and one day He will reveal Himself as the King above all kings. As Scripture tells us, He will rule as absolute sovereign. But He will always be overflowing with grace and mercy.

He is kind, patient, tender, loving, forgiving, and gracious. I can fall in love with such a person, can't you?

So here is the question. How then shall we *respond* to this great God, who is so severe yet so kind? How can we *celebrate* both God's kindness and His severity? Or, how do we *approach* such a God? How do we love and serve Him with all our heart, all our soul, and all our strength? Permit me to share several appropriate responses from Scripture.

Let Us Respect Him and Honor Him as Holy

It is a fearful thing to fall into the hands of the living God. (Heb. 10:31)

Princess Diana's tragic death on August 31, 1997, and each anniversary of it revived the memory of her momentous wedding. St. Paul's Cathedral was filled with the rich, the famous, and the powerful, while an estimated 750 million people watched on television. It was billed as the "wedding of the century."

I remember an entertaining newspaper article in *The Oregonian* seeking to give a little context to American observers. Speaking of the deference that Brits give to their royal family, the writer said: "You just don't walk up to His Royal Highness Prince Charles Arthur George, Prince of Wales, KG, KT, GCB, OM, AK, QSO, PC, ADC, Earl of Chester, Duke of Rothesay, Earl of Carrick, Baron of Renfrew, Lord of the Isles and Prince and Great Steward of Scotland and say, 'Hi ya, Chuck.'"[9]

You can call me Syd, Pastor, Preach, brother, or almost anything. I don't have a long list of titles or credentials.

Truthfully, I welcome the informality and fresh winds of grace flowing through contemporary Christianity. In the process, however, are we in danger of failing to respect God? If I

Do I approach God as my Holy Father, or am I a fool blabbering something stupid like, "Hi ya, Pops"?

truly recognize whom I am addressing, can I casually rush into His throne room? As Alexander Pope noted, "Fools rush in where angels fear to tread."[10] Do I approach God as my Holy Father, or am I a fool blabbering something stupid like, "Hi ya, Pops"? Somehow we must recapture the balance between respecting God and enjoying His friendship and companionship.

I have been challenged by people who met God and immediately fell on their faces. Some feared for their very lives. When Isaiah heard the voices of the seraphim praising the One seated on a throne, he trembled and cried, "Woe is me!" and admitted his lips were unclean. Moses fell on his face at the burning bush; Saul fell to the ground. Should I not bow my heart, if not my knees, before Him? How often I rush into prayer without a thought about my need for confession. I am grateful we no longer live under the old bloody sacrificial system, but we must not become too casual.

Let Us Boldly Draw Near to Him without Fear or Shame

> Therefore, brothers, since we have confidence to enter the holy places by the blood of Jesus, by the new and living way that he opened for us through the curtain, that is, through his flesh, and since we have a great priest over the house of God, let us draw near with a true heart in full assurance of faith, with our hearts sprinkled clean from an evil and our bodies washed with pure water. (Heb. 10:19–22)

Jesus, our High Priest, understands us because He was (and is) one of us. When I am tempted or struggling, there is no safer place than the arms of our loving God.

In 2002, I was scheduled to minister at the Pakistan International Church in Islamabad. Just one month before my departure, however, a suicide bomber entered the church, detonating a bomb that killed five and injured forty attendees. I wondered what I could say to these broken people who had lost loved ones, limbs, or eyesight. I was strongly warned against making the trip and going through the airport in Mumbai alone. But I asked God for wisdom and the courage to go.

When I am tempted or struggling, there is no safer place than the arms of our loving God.

After ministering to persecuted Christians in India with a team from Open Doors, I left my group in New Delhi to travel alone through Mumbai with the warnings echoing in my mind. I prayed for wisdom and protection as I waited to board my flight to Mumbai. Just a few minutes before boarding time a well-dressed Indian man sat next to me in the waiting area. I asked if he was from Delhi. In perfect American English he responded, "No, I'm from San Diego." He escorted me through Mumbai and made certain I got on the correct bus. My heavenly Father heard my prayer and provided a personal escort!

You and I have received an invitation to come to God as we are without all the protocol required in the world when we meet kings and princesses. We can approach God with confidence and share our deepest concerns. We don't need to plead or grovel or use flowery words but simply talk as we would to a loving earthly father.

Let Us Praise Him for His Infinite Wisdom

Oh, the depth of the riches and wisdom and knowledge of God! How unsearchable are his judgments and how inscrutable his ways!

129

> "For who has known the mind of the Lord,
>   or who has been his counselor?"
> "Or who has given a gift to him
>   that he might be repaid?"

> For from him and through him and to him are all things.
> To him be glory forever. Amen. (Rom. 11:33–36)

The Scripture above is Paul's response of wonder and praise to a God who is both kind and severe. It's as though he reaches verse 33 and just throws his quill pen into the air, overcome with awe—and delight. He is like a child seeing his first butterfly. God is too great to be packaged in a theology book. All we can say is, "Wow! What an amazing God."

I can't help but recall the lyrics to the beautiful contemporary worship song, "I Stand in Awe of You." The tune plays in my mind along with the words, *"You are beautiful beyond description . . ."*[11] The song declares that words cannot describe Him because He is unlike anything we know or have seen.

Let Us Offer Our Lives to Serve Him

Because of all He has done for us, we can serve Him in worship and thanksgiving for His mercy and grace.

> I appeal to you therefore, brothers, by the mercies of God, to present your bodies as a living sacrifice, holy and acceptable to God, which is your spiritual worship. (Rom. 12:1)

The proper response to God's mercy and wisdom is to present all we have and all we are in sacrificial service to Him for the blessing of serving others.

Let Us Love Him with All Our Heart and Strength

"Hear, O Israel: The LORD our God, the LORD is one. You shall love the LORD your God with all your heart and with all your soul and with all your might." (Deut. 6:4–5)

God calls for Israel's full attention, "Hear [shema], O Israel." We have but one God, in three persons. He prefers to express His love and mercy, but He will unleash His wrath when appropriate. He is to be loved, and He is to be feared. Our response is to love Him passionately and trust Him fully.

So let us enjoy God, because there is no greater joy in life! Jesus said, "I came that they may have life and have it abundantly. . . . And this is eternal life, that they know you, the only true God, and Jesus Christ whom you have sent" (John 10:10; 17:3).

Eternal life is more than spending some future state with God. It is experiencing life here and now right down on the ground—to live life as it was meant to be lived. Life is more than getting up in the morning to go to work to make money to have a home to sleep in so we can get up in the morning to go to work . . .

We were meant to be more than conquerors according to Paul (Rom. 8:37). We are not wilted plants struggling to survive; in Christ we were meant to thrive.

Because God has revealed Himself in Scripture and in Jesus, life has taken on new purpose. Somebody loved me enough to rescue me. Every breath is a gift. Every delicious bite of food is a gift. Every moment of laughter is a gift. Every relationship I enjoy is a gift.

If there is a God, the two most important questions you will ever deal with are these: (1) *What is God like?* (2) *How can I know and relate to Him?* God gives us answers to these

GOD IN HIS OWN IMAGE

questions. How you answer them will influence everything you think and do. Without God in the equation, just eat, drink, and be merry because there's nothing waiting after this life. There's no judgment or reward. No heaven or hell. This is it! Someday these lungs will take their last breath and this heart will make its last beat and this warm skin will become cold.

Our greatest challenge is to know God and to enjoy Him. As the prophet Jeremiah described it,

"Let not the wise man boast in his wisdom, let not the mighty man boast in his might, let not the rich man boast in his riches, but let him who boasts boast in this, that he understands and knows me, that I am the LORD who practices steadfast love, justice, and righteousness in the earth. For in these things I delight, declares the LORD." (Jer. 9:23–24)

Drawn by His Kindness

God delights in love, justice, and righteousness. We know Him and love Him for His softer attributes like love, mercy, and grace. But without God's holiness and severe wrath, His mercy and grace are more like cheap rhinestones than spectacular diamonds. In fact, mercy loses its meaning if there is not a death sentence hanging over every sinner.

In Romans 2:3–4 Paul warns about treating God's judgment casually: "Do you suppose, O man—you who judge those who practice such things and yet do them yourself—that you will escape the judgment of God? *Or do you presume on the riches of his kindness and forbearance and patience, not knowing that God's kindness is meant to lead you to repentance?*" (emphasis mine).

Did you catch that? It is God's *kindness* that draws us to Him and brings us to repentance, turning us away from our old selfish pursuits. It is God's grace and indescribable loyal love that breaks the chains that bound us to the old love affairs. It is His loyal love and His incalculable grace that have quenched my thirst.

A nineteenth-century Scottish preacher, Thomas Chalmers, preached a sermon titled, "The Expulsive Power of a New Affection."[12] His point was that when we passionately fall in love with someone new, the old, negative love affair is no longer attractive.

Falling in love is an amazing experience. Life takes on new meaning, and our focus is concentrated on pleasing the new lover. Everyone else and everything else takes the back seat—or is kicked out of the car. That's the way it ought to be when we fall in love with Jesus.

After we have tasted God's grace and love, we always desire more.

Peter challenges his readers to "long for the pure spiritual milk, that by it you may grow up into salvation—if indeed you have tasted that the Lord is good" (1 Peter 2:2–3). After we have tasted God's grace and love, we always desire more. When I was still chained to external rules of legalism, I had little appetite for God's Word. Why? Because I had never tasted His goodness—only His severity. The gospel was merely a fire insurance policy or get-out-of-jail-free card.

I remember a man in Marion, Ohio, who boasted that he had shared the gospel with a waitress by holding a pot of hot coffee over her hand and saying, "Hell will be a lot hotter than this." I am serious. He really did that. No doubt some people have been converted by responding to a severe message about God's wrath or hell. But the gospel is *good news* that God loved me enough to rescue me at Jesus' expense. The gospel isn't a fire insurance policy. It's a love letter inviting us to be thrilled with God Himself.

I keep the insurance policies on our home and our automobiles in a file, but I never read them. On the other hand, encouraging letters are another story. Over the years of ministry, I kept a file that I called my "Blue Mondays." I kept letters of appreciation or handwritten notes about how a sermon or something I said or did had influenced somebody. When ministry got tough and the sheep began to bite, these notes encouraged me. When Mary and I were separated by more than two thousand miles during a summer break from college, I read and devoured her love letters over and over again. Every word was precious.

I can do the same with God's love letter. Thankfully the men who wrote the sixty-six books we call the Bible were common folk that I can understand. They introduce me to a God I can love.

I no longer live as one who dreads the Cosmic Cop. As I reflect on my life, I find myself saying again and again, "I am so blessed!" I enjoy a healthy marriage with an amazing woman who accepted me as I was and loved me into becoming a better man. We have friends around the world with whom we have shared life and ministry. I never worried about preparing for our retirement, but today we know God's sufficiency. We have taken several long road trips. As a simple farm boy, I never dreamed of traveling around the globe, but God has enabled me to minister in several countries.

I have tasted and discovered the Lord is good. Even if God took away everything I enjoy today, I can still testify that I have tasted His goodness. If the physician says I only have a short time to live, I have no regrets. Life has been a blessing, and the future is beyond comprehension. In reading the Psalms, I discovered a verse that describes my feelings today:

But I am like a green olive tree
    in the house of God.
I trust in the steadfast love of God
    forever and ever.
I will thank you forever,
    because you have done it.
I will wait for your name, for it is good,
    in the presence of the godly.
(Ps. 52:8–9)

Several years ago, Barbara, a woman who had zest for life and for Jesus, was diagnosed with terminal cancer. She shared her journey through pain and dying with our church family. I will always remember Barbara saying, "I want to slide into home plate in a cloud of dust." Because she had tasted that the Lord is good, she finished strong.

Chris, a member of our church, was diagnosed in May 2017 with a brain tumor and told he could only expect to live three to five months. His faith became more real and on display than ever. He knew he would leave a wife and two children, but he radiated a peace and joy. In his own words, "The old Chris had already died."

His family celebrated their last Christmas together in October 2017. In a few days, Chris released his last post on Facebook, and as I read it, I could hear Paul's words in Philippians 1:23, "My desire is to depart and be with Christ, for that is far better."

How can this confidence and peace be so real in such difficult circumstances? It is because God is good. He has given hope in the midst of pain and loss and even death. Chris accepted the invitation to taste God's goodness.

Earlier in this book, I mentioned Nabeel Qureshi, Christian

author and former Muslim. I strongly recommend his books, *Seeking Allah, Finding Jesus* and *No God but One: Allah or Jesus?* In his own words, Nabeel described his conversion as "The God of the Bible reached me through investigations, dreams, and visions, and called me to prayer in my suffering. It was there that I found Jesus. To follow him is worth giving up everything."[13] Nabeel followed Jesus faithfully.

In the spring of 2017, Nabeel was diagnosed with aggressive stomach cancer and entered into the presence of Jesus September 16, 2017. Shortly before his death, he spoke from his hospital bed in Houston and closed his video by praying for a miracle, "Please come through. If it is not Your will, I trust and I love You anyway." Nabeel had tasted and discovered our God is good.

Billy Graham passed into the presence of God on February 21, 2018. On major television networks, in an interview recorded before his death, the evangelist said he was looking forward to death because he wanted to see God face-to-face. Billy Graham had tasted and discovered that God is good. Today his thirst has been fully quenched.

I have asked God to help me present Him accurately through the pages of this book, but of course He is beyond human description. He is unlike anything we have experienced or could ever conceive. He is holy and righteous and just; He will not be trivialized. Yet, He *is* love. Unselfish, amazing love! Therefore, everything God does is done in love—even His discipline.

His love is so severe and so unselfish that His Son (who is also God) came to live and die to pay the penalty you and I deserve.

The dinner invitation remains open.

"Taste and see that the LORD is good."

Discussion Questions
for Small Groups

Preface

1. The author never had a goal to write a book. Share how you have done something that you never thought you would do.

2. What would you like to learn from reading and discussing this book?

3. Respond to the author's reference to the "older testament." Have you ever struggled with understanding or accepting the Old Testament? If so, share the reason for the struggle. Do you know anyone who considers the Old Testament to be no longer relevant?

4. The author has chosen Romans 11:22 as the theme verse of this book. Read the verse, and if you have time, all of Romans 11. Do "kindness" and "severity" seem to be in conflict to you? How can they be reconciled?

Chapter 1: *What Is God Like?*

1. Share some reasons you believe in God.

2. What difference has your faith in God made in your life?

3. Have you ever tried to manipulate or make a deal with God? How did that work out?

4. Read 1 Kings 18. What does this chapter show us about God? Where is His kindness evident? Where do you see His harshness? Is it justified? Why or why not?

5. Share an experience when you felt unjustly treated due to another person's capricious actions or their impressions about you. Have you ever been the perpetrator of such actions?

6. Psalm 19 begins, "The heavens declare the glory of God." Where does God most naturally seem to communicate with you through His creation? Is it the coast or the mountains or somewhere else? Share a time when you felt God's presence while in nature. Why do you think we are more perceptive of God's presence when we are in nature?

Chapter 2: *First Impressions*

1. Describe a time when your first impression of someone was strong and wrong. How did your wrong impression change?

2. How have your early impressions of God changed? Do you currently see Him as more loving or more stern?

3. If, like the author, legalism influenced your impressions of and your personal walk with God, how have you learned to recognize and deal with this?

4. The author used two words, *immanent* and *transcendent*, to contrast the god of pantheism with our living God, Yahweh. In your own words, share what these two words mean and how the pantheistic view differs from the biblical view of God.

5. With which attribute(s) or characteristics of God do you most readily identify? Why? Share how each of these attributes cause you to respond to God in worship and praise.

6. Read 1 Kings 20:13–25. How did Syria underestimate the God of Israel? Can you think of times or ways you have underestimated or trivialized God?

7. Have you "walked through the valley" and come out with an even stronger faith? If so, share your experience. What lessons did you learn through that difficult experience?

8. Tragic or painful experiences may influence, even distort, our view of God. For example, Charles Templeton, one-time friend and associate with Billy Graham, denounced his faith and declared himself to be an agnostic. Have you ever struggled balancing your faith in the midst of painful experiences or observing the random suffering around you? If you presently face unexplainable suffering, with whom can you share your struggle and seek support?

Chapter 3: *From Prince of Egypt to Friend of God*

1. God dramatically revealed Himself to Moses at the burning bush. How has God revealed Himself to us?

2. Read Exodus 3:1–12. What did Moses learn about God in this passage? What do you learn about God? How is this knowledge frightening? In what ways is it comforting?

3. What does God's identity as "I AM WHO I AM" mean to you? How has it influenced you?

4. Aaron made a golden calf, resulting in Israel losing focus on the true God. What are some of the "golden calves" that may distract us from keeping our eyes and lives centered on God?

5. Moses spent forty years living in solitude as a shepherd before he met God at the burning bush. How important are times of solitude and quietness for maintaining a healthy spiritual life?

6. Moses and Joshua began to meet "face-to-face" with God in the Tent of Meeting. Where is your preferred place of solitude to meet with God? Or do you struggle with experiencing quiet times alone with God?

7. Respond to John Piper's statement that "God's anger must be released by a stiff safety latch, but his mercy has a hair trigger." Does Piper's description of God's mercy and anger mesh with your early opinion about God?

Chapter 4: *Kindness and Severity: Where They Meet*

1. The author has based the entire book on two words, *kindness* and *severity*, found in Romans 11:22. Which of these attributes of God was more dominant in your early religious training and experience? How have your impressions of God changed over time?

2. How difficult is it for you to accept that God has a severe, even wrathful, side to His nature? Share how this chapter did or did not help you appreciate the fullness of God's character and attributes.

3. Unbelieving Israel was "cut off" to allow the Gentiles to be grafted in. What had Israel done to deserve being

so severely cut off? How does the truth about grafting in Gentiles relate to you? Discuss Paul's warning that Gentiles must not become proud lest God cut us off also. What might cutting off a person look like?

4. Many people struggle with seeing the God of the older and newer testaments as the same God. Read Isaiah 49:15–16 and Romans 8:37–39. In what ways are these two passages similar? How does God express His commitment to His people in these texts?

5. Respond to the statement: "The opposite of anger is not love but apathy." Share a perceived injustice that has caused you to experience "righteous anger." Share your strategy to confront this injustice.

6. The author stated that the word *kindness* is not a verb, but it is an action word. Share some examples of "grace in action" you have personally experienced or witnessed in your church or small group. Share an experience when you were personally encouraged through receiving "grace in action."

7. Respond to the statement that both the severe hurricanes and the resulting outpouring of compassion and assistance were acts of God. Why do you think it takes disasters to bring people together?

Chapter 5: *Lion and Lamb*

1. What did your mental image of Jesus look like before reading this chapter?

2. The author shared occasions when Jesus demonstrated His "lion" side in the Gospels. Share other examples of Jesus acting like the Lion from Scripture.

3. Read Revelation 6:12–16. Who is described here as expressing "wrath"? How is this a surprising image? Read Revelation 19:11–16. How is this image different from what we read of Jesus in the Gospels? How is it consistent with those accounts?

4. G. Campbell Morgan described God seeking Adam and Eve in the garden as "the wail of a father, who had lost his child." How does Campbell's perspective of Adam and Eve's experience compare with the way you have previously viewed the story of God seeking Adam and Eve in the garden?

5. God's judgment upon the entire human race was demonstrated in the great flood. Respond to the charge that God was not righteous or fair by destroying innocent children.

6. Critics challenge the claim that God is love and always acts in a loving manner by asking, "How can God be love when He commanded Israel to kill thousands of people, including women and children?" Have you ever struggled with the same question? (*Note:* The appendix deals more thoroughly with this question. After you've read the appendix, consider: In your opinion, does the author provide a legitimate response to the charge God is not good if He commanded the army of Israel to kill women and children?)

7. Revelation contains several descriptions of corporate worship, including examples of God being praised for His wrath and justice. Since worship is a response to God's character and works, why do we find it so difficult and why do we so rarely praise Him when He carries out justice on the earth?

Chapter 6: *Is God Unfair?*

1. After studying this chapter, share examples from your own experience or from your observations of inherited or learned sins being passed from one generation to another.

2. What cultural sins are being experienced by succeeding generations today? How are these sins being acted out in your community?

3. Was God right (righteous) to punish Achan's whole family for the sin he committed? Share why you feel that way? (*Note:* The appendix deals more thoroughly with the judgment upon Achan's family.)

4. We often associate wrath with the Old Testament image of God. But Acts 5, telling the story of Ananias and Sapphira, is in the newer testament. Read Acts 5:1–11. How does this event add to our view of the fullness of God?

5. Note this description of God's anger: "God's wrath is not a cranky explosion, but his settled opposition to the cancer of sin, which is eating out the insides of the human race he loves with his whole being." How does this description help in understanding or explaining God's severe response to sin?

6. This chapter lists ACEs (Adverse Childhood Experiences) that hurt children. How prevalent are these experiences in your community? Your church? Your extended family? Share how you, personally or as a small group, can help make a difference in the lives of children caught in these negative situations.

7. If you were raised in a negative home environment where you experienced some of the ACEs listed in the book, how has it affected you? If you have experienced healing, share what and/or who has helped make the difference and bring about healing in your life.

Chapter 7: *Taste and See*

1. The author quotes from an article in *Christianity Today*: "Life is complex. God is not." What was the author of the quote getting at? What does it mean that God is simple, not complex?

2. How would you rank your priorities in life? Do you struggle balancing the demands on your life?

3. G. Campbell Morgan is quoted as saying, "The reason for man's fear is not in God; it is in man." Do you agree? What lingering fears about God do you have that you can release to Him?

4. Psalm 34:8 invites us to "taste" God and experience His goodness. What does this mean? Describe your search to know God and your experience when you discovered He was inviting you to share a personal relationship with Him. How would you describe your relationship with God? Is it growing? What do you intend to do to deepen the relationship?

5. The author shared how God's choices for his life were always better than what he had originally intended to do. For example, the author planned to attend seminary after earning his BA degree. In hindsight, God's plan for Syd to assume the pastorate of a small country

church proved to be much better. Share examples from your own experience of how God has led in your life.

6. Read Psalm 27. What are a few things the psalmist requests of God? What are some of his greatest longings? How do these compare with the deepest longings of your own heart?

7. Sometimes following Jesus may result in suffering or death as a martyr. How can we resolve these apparent exceptions that God always gives the best to those who leave the choice to Him?

Appendix

**How can God be righteous if He commanded Israel
to kill women and children when they conquered the
Promised Land?**

The above question was submitted by Josh, a twentysomething
millennial who read the manuscript. The following information
is a response to the sixth discussion question in chapter 5.

At first, I thought the question might be too difficult since
the book has been addressed to the average layperson rather
than to the seminarian or pastor. After more thought, I realized
the question is ground zero to the discussion. If I can't respond
to this question about God's fairness, then everything in the
book has been rendered null and void. If God is not good and
righteous or if He does what is wrong and unfair, then why
should I love Him or serve Him? If God is malevolent and
cruel, He is no better than the idols men and women have created in their own image.

I have tried to resolve the quandary created by God's command for Israelite soldiers to kill women and children when
they conquered the land from the Canaanites. For your consid-
eration, I offer five principles gleaned primarily from Genesis
and Deuteronomy.

To better appreciate the book of Deuteronomy, try to
imagine a marriage ceremony between God and Israel taking
place in Moab prior to crossing the Jordan River to claim their
promised inheritance.

Imagine an old patriarch having counted 120 summers and

winters. There he stands, weathered physically by the elements and emotionally from the stress of leading a bunch of rebels who have resisted his leadership at almost every point along the journey. Every person twenty and older, minus two men and their families, has perished in the Sinai Desert. The new generation is being instructed about the blessings and curses in the covenant. Moses is the marriage counselor or pastor preparing the new generation who will enter into a covenant with Yahweh. Since this is the second time Israel would enter into the covenant, it was more like a renewal of marriage vows after adultery.

So, let's consider the five principles:

Principle #1: The issue is more about God's nature than about an apparent atrocity being carried out against "innocent" persons.

God is absolutely sovereign. He is the One True King who rules over every earthly king! He raises up and removes whomever He pleases.

David ruled over Israel, but he always knew the only truly sovereign ruler was Yahweh. Consider David's words from Psalm 22:28: "For kingship belongs to the LORD, and he rules over the nations."

Sometimes God specifically claims His sovereign right to rule simply because this is His world. As Creator, He owns the title deed to the universe. In the words of an old hymn, "This is my Father's world." Since this is His world, He is the absolute Supreme Judge, and the universe is His jurisdiction and heaven His courtroom. He determines what is right or wrong—just or unjust.

I have a friend, who wishes to remain anonymous, that

describes it this way: God is the Alpha and Omega, and He doesn't change like shifting shadows. He loves the world in 2019 as much as ever, but He doesn't have to tip His hat to political correctness, and it isn't our job to try to adapt His standards to fit the mindset of our times.

Let me illustrate from my experience growing up on a wheat farm. When my father and mother were married, Dad bought the farm that had belonged to my mother's family. As a result of several adverse situations, including the death of my grandfather, the farm was up for sale. After my father purchased the farm, the title deed changed from John Kahrs, my grandfather, to Gerald Brestel. It was now Dad's farm to do with as he chose.

I grew up on the farm loving the land, exploring the fields, and playing in the barn. But when my father became a pastor, we moved to town. My father rented the land to be farmed by someone else. It remained my dad's farm, but the new tenants were managing it. They could pretty much do as they wished with the farm. But my father had one absolute rule: "Do not farm my land on Sundays." Whether anybody agreed with that rule or not is irrelevant. It was Dad's land, and he could set the rules controlling the use of it.

I understand why most farmers harvest on Sundays. One hailstorm can destroy the entire crop. In less than a half hour, a year's income can be pounded into the soil. So when the wheat is ripe, everything else takes second place to gathering in the harvest. Even on Sundays.

During harvest one hot July Sunday afternoon, a combine caught fire, resulting in the loss of a significant portion of the wheat crop. Obviously, my father found out. Since the order not to farm his land on Sundays had been violated, my father took the right to farm the land away from the tenants.

Was Dad fair? Yes, because it was his land! Farming on Sunday may not have broken some irrevocable law, nor did it make the tenants evil or wicked. They simply ignored the rule Dad had set down for managing his land.

I share that crude illustration as a reminder that God has the right (and the wisdom) to determine what is right or righteous. This is His world, so He sets the rules and determines right from wrong. Just from unjust. It is not mine to question Him or to challenge His rules. It is mine to trust Him to always do what is right because of His character. I may not understand or feel comfortable with everything God commands, but I trust Him to know and do what is right in every situation.

Several Old Testament passages support the claim that God raises up and removes empires to accomplish His will and to carry out His sentence against them. Consider Micah 4:11–13 and Ezekiel 25:12–14. The text that nails it down for me is Habakkuk 1:5, where God shocks the prophet with these words, "For I am doing a work in your days that you would not believe if told." God was raising up cruel, vicious Babylon to discipline His own people, Judah.

Jeremiah prophesied during a perilous time. His messages brought persistent warnings Babylon would invade Judah. Many would be slaughtered while others would be carried away into exile. One day, God told Jeremiah to visit the potter's house where God would give the prophet a sermon illustration. You can read about it in Jeremiah 18:1–11.

Watching the potter forming a utensil out of the clay only to abandon it and begin to shape something different, Jeremiah caught the message from the Lord. "Then the word of the Lord came to me: 'O house of Israel, can I not do with you as this potter has done? declares the Lord. Behold, like the clay in the potter's hand, so are you in my hand.'"

Paul, reflecting on Jeremiah's message, wrote in Romans 9:20–21, "Who are you, O man, to answer back to God? Will what is molded say to its molder, 'Why have you made me like this?' Has the Potter no right over the clay . . . ?'"

So when it comes to God's command to annihilate an entire civilization of Canaanites, including women and children, I assume God must have had valid reasons that you and I may not understand.

Principle #2: The command to kill every occupant in the Promised Land was rooted in God's covenant with Abraham.

God appeared to Abraham several times in the book of Genesis. I believe we will discover evidence relevant to our discussion as we consider a couple of these.

Genesis 12:1–9 is the first time God appeared to Abram, while he was still a worshiper of idols. God eventually changed Abram's name to Abraham. After revealing Himself as the one true God He told Abram to leave his family, his country, and everything familiar and go to a land that God would show him. God also promised to make Abram into a great nation and to "bless those who bless you and to curse those who curse you."

The second time God appeared to Abram, who was now getting well along in age and still had no son to claim the promises God had made, is recorded in Genesis 15. Abram offered his trusted servant to be the legal heir, but God promised that a son, not a servant, would be the heir through whom many descendants would come.

God also revealed that Abraham's descendants would live in bondage four hundred years in a foreign country, where they would become a great nation before actually inheriting the

Promised Land. The long delay was not only to provide time for Abraham's descendants to grow into a sizeable nation, but the four-hundred-year delay was primarily because the "iniquity of the Amorites is not yet complete" (Gen. 15:13–16). Those were God's words. That final statement about the sin of the Amorites is a key to understanding God's command to kill every person living in the Promised Land. The people living in the land had chosen to pursue a path that would eventually (four centuries after Abraham) result in their complete destruction.

This account in Genesis 15, reaffirming the covenant that had been made in Genesis 12, is unusual—even mysterious. Several animals were slaughtered and the carcasses split in half. Usually, in this type of ancient covenant, both parties entering into the covenant walked together between the carcasses. It was like a visual threat and a promise. Each person swore to keep the covenant or they would become "dead meat" like the carcasses.

However, in this case, God put Abram into a deep sleep while He, God, the primary party in this covenant, walked alone between the carcasses, demonstrating that He alone was responsible to fulfill the conditions of the covenant. It was unilateral and irrevocable! Using contemporary slang, Abram could "take it to the bank" because God had sworn to keep His promise.

The last words recorded in Genesis 15:17–21 were part of God's promise to give the land of Canaan and all its inhabitants to Abraham's descendants.

I want to emphasize the previous statement. God, the Creator and owner of the world and all its land mass, was turning the title deed of Canaan over to Abraham's descendants, because the current tenants had become so wicked—so abominable—that God had already planned to eradicate them from the face of the earth. The Judge had already pronounced sentence against them.

Fair? Righteous? That is for God to determine, not me.

So we ask, what had the Amorites done to deserve such severe response from God?

Principle #3: The justification for the total annihilation of the Amorites is rooted in the sin of idolatry.

I believe the severe consequences of idolatry are addressed more thoroughly in Deuteronomy than any other place in the Bible. Idolatry, left unchecked, is a deadly cancer cell that will eventually destroy an entire civilization.

Moses frequently warned against idolatry in the early chapters of Deuteronomy. The lengthy dialogue between Moses and the new generation included frequent instructions. It was a three-way conversation. In my study of these chapters, so that I could more readily identify when God was speaking or when Moses or the people were speaking, I highlighted God's words in red. It may be the first "Red Letter Edition of the Old Testament."

I discovered God's reason for removing, even annihilating, the Amorites and Canaanites and all the other "ites" was based upon the promise that God had made to Abram in Genesis 15. Four hundred years had passed—sufficient time for the Amorites to repent and worship the one true God. Instead, as God had predicted, they had continued to spiral deeper into depravity. If God rules the world and all its inhabitants, can He not declare who is guilty and worthy of death? Can we trust Him to exercise capital punishment judiciously?

In Deuteronomy 1–11, Moses repeatedly reminded the Israelites that God had promised Abraham, Isaac, and Jacob to give the land and its inhabitants to Israel.

God not only promised to give the land to Israel; He also

warned Israel to never turn to idols lest they lose the privilege of living in the land (Deut. 4:14–40). Moses reminded Israel, in Deuteronomy 6:10–11, they would inherit cities they did not build and orchards they did not plant. But in the same breath, Moses warned Israel to never forget the Lord who had delivered them from bondage. Forgetting the Lord clearly included serving other gods. "You shall not go after other gods, the gods of the people who are around you—for the Lord your God is a jealous God—lest the anger of the Lord your God be kindled against you, and he destroy you from off the face of the earth" (Deut. 6:14–15).

Did you catch that warning? If Israel, God's chosen people, ever turned away from Him to serve (love) idols, the Lord their God would remove them from the face of the earth! God threatened to carry out the same discipline against Israel that He was preparing to mete out against the Amorites. This is not the only time this warning was leveled against Israel.

The history of Israel is replete with evidence God will not share His glory with a lesser being and would remove Israel from the land if they pursued other gods. Consider two examples.

First, because of rampant idolatry, the ten northern tribes were conquered by the Assyrians. It was a blood bath. Those who survived the invasion were either dispersed throughout the empire to lose their national identity or left in the land to intermarry with imported foreigners and become the hated Samaritans.

Later, Babylon laid siege against Jerusalem. To appreciate this tragedy, read the book of Lamentations through the eyes and the heart of a mother watching her infant being ripped away from her bosom, swung by the feet, and its little skull being crushed against the pavement. And we ask, "Why did

God permit this to happen to His chosen people, Judah?" It was because *God hates idolatry*. In this case, it involved His own redeemed people who, as a nation, stood by the Jordan River in Moab and publicly and corporately recited their vows to their true Lover—to Yahweh—while heaven and earth stood by as witnesses. There, by the Jordan, Israel swore total allegiance to Yahweh, promising to forsake all other gods and to love only Yahweh with *all* their heart, with *all* their soul, and with *all* their might. This is another way of saying they promised to forsake all other potential lovers, to love nobody else, and to obey the Lord God forever.

The judgment upon Achan's family that we considered back in chapter 6 is relevant here. In Deuteronomy 7:22–26, God had promised to "clear away these nations." But Moses also warned Israel,

And he [God] will give their kings into your hand, and you shall make their name perish from under heaven. No one shall be able to stand against you until you have destroyed them. *The carved images of their gods you shall burn with fire. You shall not covet the silver or the gold that is on them or take it for yourselves, lest you be ensnared by it, for it is an abomination to the Lord your God. And you shall not bring an abominable thing into your house and become devoted to destruction like it.* You shall utterly detest and abhor it, for it is devoted to destruction. (vv. 24–26, emphasis mine)

Whenever we read about Achan's sin and the sentence pronounced against him and his family, it is imperative to remember the above warning against taking a Canaanite idol that had been destined for destruction by fire. Achan and his family and possessions were burned along with the stolen treasures from

Jericho. The basis for determining the sentence against Achan had already been made back in Deuteronomy.

God plays no favorites. He always does what He has determined to be right or righteous.

Principle # 4: The offense of the sin of idolatry is rooted in its attack against the very nature of God.

Why, we may ask, is idolatry so offensive that God would destroy an entire civilization?

First, idolatry exchanges something that is eternal, the glory of God, for something temporary and trivial. A cheap replica. No other sin is such a direct insult and frontal assault against God's nature and character.

Remember the illustration from chapter 4, "Is God Unfair?" of looking at the ceiling of the Sistine Chapel and saying, "Look, some kids scribbled on the ceiling!" This would insult the great artist, Michelangelo. How much greater the insult of calling a snake or a cow or the moon, God!

If God is the Creator of the entire universe, then all praise belongs to Him. This is what Paul declared in Romans 1:18–32. The pagans were guilty because they had been surrounded by evidence of the Creator. Yet they were not grateful but began worshiping images of created things. Therefore, God gave them over to pursue foolishness, resulting in their ultimate condemnation. In other words, they condemned themselves by their choices and actions.

Several older testament prophets ridiculed the practice of bowing down before a lifeless statue instead of the living God. Try to imagine the contrast between those two images. A lifeless statue or the living God.

"With whom can we compare God?" That was Isaiah's

question in 40:18–23. How can we compare the God who has created everything with an idol that can't move or see or hear? Isaiah described Yahweh as the sovereign, transcendent God existing beyond our galaxy. In contrast with Him, we appear as grasshoppers. How can an insect even be compared to the majestic Creator?

We grow tired and weary; He gives power to finish strong. He sets up political leaders and removes them. All the nations are but a tiny drop in a large bucket compared with God.

I love the scene in the movie *The Chariots of Fire*, as Eric Liddell reads the above passage from Isaiah to a congregation in Paris on a Sunday morning while Olympic athletes are stumbling and failing to finish their races. Liddell's convictions did not permit him to run on Sunday even though his heat had been scheduled for a Sunday morning. Liddell's calm voice reading words like not fainting or growing weary are contrasted with scenes of competitors straining and coming up short.

God twice throws down the gauntlet in Isaiah 41 when He declares that He alone is the first and the last—the eternal One: "Who has performed and done this, calling the generations from the beginning? I, the Lord, the first, and with the last; I am He" (v. 4).

I am drawn by those words, "I am He," back to the burning bush where God introduced Himself to Moses.

Once again, "Thus says the Lord, the King of Israel and his Redeemer, the Lord of hosts: 'I am the first and I am the last; besides me there is no god. Who is like me? Let him proclaim it. Let him declare and sit before me'" (Isa. 44:6–8).

Imagine some puny man carrying his stone idol and accepting that challenge!

Isaiah also heaps ridicule by pointing out how ludicrous to compare something human hands have made, and that will someday be tossed into the city dump, with the eternal, sovereign Creator. How ridiculous to clap hands or strike a large cymbal to awaken a god who can't hear.

There are no imitations of God. To worship anyone or anything else is an insult to Him. God simply will not share His glory with another. He is jealous in the proper sense of the word. Idolatry is spiritual adultery, and God, a loyal husband, will not tolerate it.

It is easy to ridicule idol worship. However, idolatry is not a laughing matter because of what it does to those who worship them.

This is illustrated in Psalm 106. The psalm begins with a call to praise God "for He is good, for His steadfast love endures forever." Praise dramatically transitions to confession in verse 6. The psalmist is confessing the corporate sins of Israel. Note the charge of idolatry—the gold calf—and its consequence in verses 19–23. Only Moses's bold intercession on behalf of Israel spared the nation from total destruction on the spot.

The consequence of Israel's infatuation with idols continues in verse 34 through verse 39.

> They did not destroy the peoples,
> as the LORD commanded them,
> but they mixed with the nations
> and learned to do as they did.
> They served their idols,
> which became a snare to them.
> *They sacrificed their sons*
> *and their daughters to the demons;*
> *they poured out innocent blood,*
> *the blood of their sons and daughters,*

whom they sacrificed to the idols of Canaan,
    and the land was polluted with blood.
Thus they became unclean by their acts,
    and played the whore in their deeds. (emphasis mine)

Idolatry will defile an entire civilization. These non-gods always display the capricious and malevolent nature of their worshipers. We become like that which we worship. Israel was no exception.

Moses concluded his speech in Deuteronomy 32:15–43 by predicting Israel would pay a severe price if they failed to carry out the command to destroy all the people living in the land. Both the northern kingdom of Israel and the southern kingdom of Judah became infected with idolatry after being exposed to the Canaanites they had failed to destroy as per God's command.

Idolatry is not limited to the older testament. It would be profitable to consider warnings against idolatry in Colossians 3:5–8. Clearly there are other ways, besides literally bowing down to a statue, to serve idols.

Principle #5: Such violent warfare was not Israel's standard operating procedure.

Total annihilation of every being was not the standard operating procedure for Israel's army. Instead, Moses's instructions in Deuteronomy 20 clearly stated that the army was to approach a city and offer peace terms before laying siege against it. If peace terms were rejected, then Israel was to attack with full force but spare the women, children, and livestock. This was how Israel was to treat cities outside the borders of the Promised Land. The army of Israel was also forbidden to destroy natural resources such as forests during a siege because God cares about His land.

So, in conclusion, the command to "annihilate" all the inhabitants, including women and children, was limited specifically to the Amorites and Canaanites that had polluted the land with idolatry, creating a culture so perverted God had sentenced them to destruction. Israel was His tool to execute the sentence. God assumed full responsibility for the total defeat of the Amorites.

When I don't understand everything God does or commands, I choose to trust Him because I know His character. Consider again the words of Jeremiah 9:23–24:

> Thus says the LORD: "Let not the wise man boast in his wisdom, let not the mighty man boast in his might, let not the rich man boast in his riches, but let him who boasts boast in this, that he understands and knows me, that I am the LORD who practices steadfast love, justice, and righteousness in the earth. For in these things I delight, declares the LORD."

Acknowledgments

This book would never exist without the support and encouragement of others. Of one thing I am certain: it has not been an exercise in futility because throughout the process I have experienced moments of an almost overwhelming sense of God's presence and pleasure. It was His great mercy and love that first drew me to Him and set me free to truly live and to thrive! I have tasted and discovered the Lord is very good. Not unto me, but unto You, O Lord, be the glory!

Mary, without your encouragement and your confidence in me I would never have begun the manuscript. I remember the times you poked your head in the room and announced, with a smile, "The office is closed and dinner is served." Thank you for offering constructive criticism balanced with words of encouragement. Thank you for fifty-three years of faithfully keeping every word of the vows we made to each other. In the words of your other "favorite pastor," Father Tim in The Mitford series, "How much the wife is dearer than the bride." I cherish you and thank God for bringing you into my life. You are living evidence that God gives the best to those who leave the choice to Him.

Attempting to write a book has been a journey not unlike trekking to the summit of South Sister, one of our nearby Cascade peaks. I am so grateful for Larry Libby, who has been the guide that I needed to keep me on the trail and encourage me to keep putting one foot in front of the other until we reached the summit. Larry, I value our friendship and the memories of serving as your pastor and now having you as my editor.

Thank you for believing in me and encouraging me to tackle the challenge of writing this book. Thank you for taking the rough manuscript and making ordinary words live. How can I ever repay you for sharing your exceptional gift and creativity?

Thank you, Lynne Hilderband and Carol Randstad, for offering suggestions and correcting grammar and discovering mixed metaphors. Your positive comments helped spur me on. Lynne, the discussion questions you wrote will help make the book more practical. Carol, your comments on the relevancy of the subject matter helped assure me the project was not in vain.

Mark Hoeffner and Andy Baxter, your theological insights and practical comments improved the original manuscript both in content and readability. Thank you.

Michael Long, your skill in formatting the text were invaluable, saving me hours of laborious struggle.

Troll, my hiking buddy, you have been an encourager throughout the process of writing the book. Thank you for letting me share a little bit of your story. Your quiet, but crystal-clear faith has enriched my life in ways you may never understand. Yes, "This is the day the LORD has made; let us rejoice and be glad in it" (Ps. 118:24). It's all about You, Jesus, and the Holy Spirit who dwells within. Amen!

I am deeply grateful to Moody Publishers for considering the manuscript to be relevant and for accepting the risk of publishing an unknown author who never intended to write a book.

Notes

Preface

1. Dean William Ralph Inge, *More Lay Thoughts of Dean* (London and New York: Putnam, 1931), 201. The full quote reads: "There are two kinds of fools. One says, 'This is old, therefore it is good.' The other says, 'This is new, therefore it is better.'"
2. A. W. Tozer, *The Pursuit of God* (1948; repr., Chicago: Moody Publishers, 2015), 13.
3. Ibid.

Chapter 1: What Is God Like?

1. Timothy Keller, *The Reason for God, Belief in an Age of Reason* (New York: Dutton, 2008), 71.
2. Richard Rodgers, "Something Good," in *The Sound of Music* (film), 1965.
3. Bob Smietana, "Most Churchgoers Say God Wants Them to Prosper Financially," LifeWay Research, July 31, 2018, https://lifewayresearch .com/2018/07/31/most-churchgoers-say-god-wants-them-to-prosper-financially/.
4. Paul Marcerelli was the character for this television commercial for Verizon Wireless until 2001.

Chapter 2: First Impressions

1. Zondervan Music Publishers, "O Be Careful Little Eyes," public domain.
2. Nabeel Qureshi, *No God But One: Allah or Jesus?* (Grand Rapids: Zondervan, 2016), 61.
3. Ibid., 62.
4. Heinrich Hein, 1797–1856, German essayist, poet and author who was influenced by the writings of Hegel and was a distant relative of Karl Marx. He lived an irreligious and immoral lifestyle but claimed to return to "religion" on his "Mattress-Grave," the name he gave the bed where he would spend the last eight years of his life.
5. Lee Strobel, *The Case for Faith* (Grand Rapids: Zondervan, 2000), 16–22.
6. Peter Hitchens, *The Rage Against God* (Grand Rapids: Zondervan, 2010), 20.
7. Ibid., 149.
8. Ibid., 150, Hitchens is quoting Thomas Nagel, professor at New York University, *The Last Word* (New York: Oxford University Press, 2001).
9. Lyrics by Annie Johnson Flint, 1866–1932; music by Alfred B. Smith, 1916–2001, "God Hath Not Promised," public domain.

Chapter 3: From Prince of Egypt to Friend of God

1. Read Exodus 2:11–22 and Acts 7:20–29.

2. God's self-disclosure appears in total or part in the following passages: Ex. 34:5–7; Num. 14:18; Deut. 5:9–10; 2 Chron. 30:9; Neh. 9:17; Pss. 86:15; 103:17; 111:1–4; 112:4; 116:5; 145:8; Jer. 32:18–19; Joel 2:13; Jonah 4:2; Nah. 1:3.

3. John Piper, *The Pleasures of God: Meditations on God's Delight in Being God* (Colorado Springs: Multnomah Books, 2008), 185.

Chapter 4: Kindness and Severity: Where They Meet

1. C. S. Lewis, *The Lion, the Witch and the Wardrobe* (1950; repr., New York: HarperCollins, 2008), 79–80.

2. John Newton, "Amazing Grace," public domain.

3. John Wesley, "Amazing Love," public domain.

4. James Hope Moulton and George Milligan, *The Vocabulary of the Greek Testament* (Grand Rapids: Wm. B. Eerdmans Publishing Company, 1930), 71.

Chapter 5: Lion and Lamb

1. Lela Long, "Jesus Is the Sweetest Name I Know," public domain.

2. G. Campbell Morgan, *Great Chapters of the Bible* (London: Marshall, Morgan & Scott, 1972), 25.

3. John Piper, *The Pleasures of God: Meditations on God's Delight in Being God* (Colorado Springs: Multnomah Books, 2008), 185.

4. Peter Hitchens, *The Rage Against God* (Grand Rapids: Zondervan, 2010), 134–35.

Chapter 6: Is God Unfair?

1. Timothy Keller, *The Reason for God, Belief in an Age of Reason* (New York: Dutton, 2008), 73.

2. Record of the Week: RCA's Disk by Ames Spins Poignant Message of Today (Billboard, December 2, 1967), 3.

3. Ed Ames, "Who Will Answer?," RCA Victor.

4. Examples of O.T. passages condemning idolatry include Ex. 34:17; Deut. 5:9; 32:16, 21; and Josh. 24:19–20.

5. The origin of this quote is unknown. It has been attributed to Becky Pippert, *Hope Has Its Reasons,* but is not found in either edition of that book.

6. J. D. Vance, *Hillbilly Elegy* (New York: HarperCollins Publishers, 2016), 226.

Chapter 7: Taste and See

1. "The Origin of 'Proof Is in the Pudding,'" NPR, August 24, 2012, https://www.npr.org/2012/08/24/159975466/corrections-and-comments-to-stories.

2. Derek Rishmawy, "Life Is Complex. God Is Not," *Christianity Today*, July/August 2017, 24.

3. Ibid.

4. G. Campbell Morgan, *Great Chapters of the Bible* (London: Marshall, Morgan & Scott, 1979), 25.

5. *Westminster Shorter Catechism*, Westminster Assembly, 1647–1648.

6. A. W. Tozer, *The Pursuit of God* (1948; repr., Chicago: Moody Publishers, 2015), 22.

7. Ibid., 21.

8. William J. Gaither, "The Longer I Serve Him," 1965.

9. *The Oregonian*, Portland, OR.

10. Alexander Pope, *Essay on Criticism*; public domain, first published in 1711. (Pope, an English poet, lived 1688–1744.)

11. Mark Altrogge, "I Stand in Awe of You" (Sovereign Grace Praise, BMI, 1986).

12. Thomas Chalmers, *The Expulsive Power of a New Affection*, public domain (Chalmers, 1787–1847, Scottish preacher and professor at the University of Edinburgh, preached this sermon based on 1 John 2:15. The sermon has been reprinted and is available on Kindle).

13. Nabeel Qureshi, "Jesus Called Me Off the Minaret," *Christianity Today*, January/February 2014, 96.

"WHAT IS GOD LIKE?"

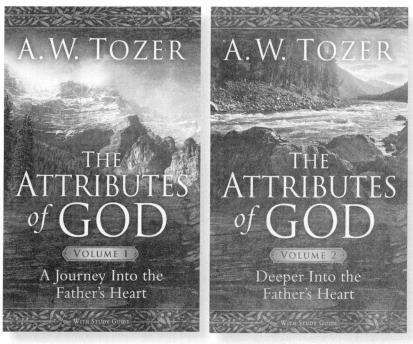

978-1-60066-129-7   978-1-60066-791-6

IS YOUR CHURCH TRANSFORMING THE COMMUNITY?

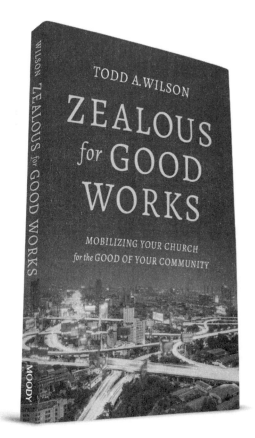

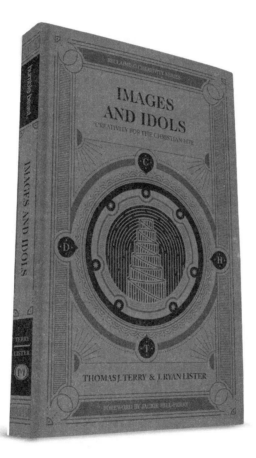

DOES YOUR CHURCH FEEL LIKE FAMILY?

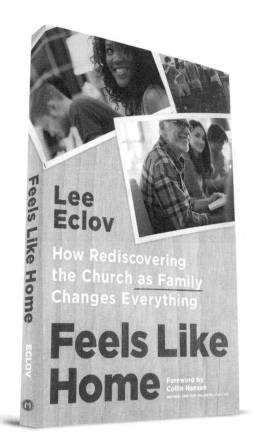

Feels Like Home is a call to pastors to return to the simplicity and profundity of the New Testament teachings about the church as a family—to focus more on creating a safe environment than a productive enterprise. Lee Eclov has been a pastor for over 40 years and spent many of those years thinking through and working out these principles. God made us a family, it's time to start living like we believe it.

978-0-8024-1886-9 | also available as an eBook